WHO YOU CaLLiN' CuPCaKe?

WHO YOU CALLIN' CUPCAKE?

75 IN-YOUR-FACE RECIPES
THAT REINVENT THE CUPCAKE

Michelle Garcia
Vinny Garcia

Ulysses Press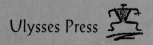

Published by Ulysses Press
       P.O. Box 3440
       Berkeley, CA 94703
       www.ulyssespress.com

ISBN: 978-1-56975-739-0
Library of Congress Catalog Number 2009930131

Printed in China by Everbest Printing through Four Colour Print Group

10 9 8 7 6 5 4 3 2 1

Acquisitions Editor: Nick Denton-Brown
Managing Editor: Claire Chun
Editor: Lauren Harrison
Proofreader: Lily Chou
Production: Judith Metzener
Design: what!design @ whatweb.com
Photos: © Bill Lambert

Distributed by Publishers Group West

For everyone who has supported Bleeding Heart.
You know who you are.

Table of Contents

WORLD TOUR

BLUE PLATE SPECIAL

FARM TO TABLE 123

CHOC-O-MATIC 143

I WANT CANDY 161

SHUT YOUR PIE HOLE 177

INTRODUCtioN

For years in the food business, I was a very complicated pastry chef—I was duped into believing you needed thousands of gadgets and every cookbook under the sun to make anything taste good. That was crazy talk.

I chose to write this book to save you time and money. Every recipe was chosen to show you how many uses you can get by changing just the littlest detail in a basic recipe. You can even make these cupcakes vegan without breaking a sweat! Even if you don't use these specific cupcake and frosting recipes, the point I'm trying to express is to keep it simple. All you need is a few basic recipes you know are fail safe, and anything is possible.

Inspiration for my flavor combinations comes from everywhere: dinner at an amazing restaurant, walking around Chicago, taking a ride to get milk for my kids, and sometimes even from a dream or a joke. You can draw inspiration from anything, it's just up to you to make something from it. Now, not everything will turn out to be spectacular—I've certainly had a few massive failures (think gin and juice with an herb topping)—but I always learn and move onward and upward!

I still keep all my cookbooks around, but really, they're just to make me look smart. In my pocket I keep a little notebook with just under a dozen recipes that have become the roots of everything I do in the kitchen. Most of the cupcakes in this book are the result of playing around with my core recipes. But in the first chapter, Anarchy in the Cupcake Pan, you'll find those basic cupcakes, frostings, and toppings that, with a little tweaking, you can make into something awesome.

aNARCHY iN THE cUpcaKe PAN

★★★★★

Vanilla Bean Cupcakes

For years we made classic European-style butter cake. Personally, I loved it; it was rich and buttery. However, it dried out quickly and we knew that we had to find an alternative. So many customers came in asking me for white cake, but I never really knew what flavor "white" was, so vanilla bean was the answer. This recipe uses a different mixing method than most and bakes quickly, but it stays moist and lends itself well as a base for other recipes.

1⅔ cups sugar

1⅔ cups all-purpose flour

1 tablespoon baking powder

1½ teaspoons salt

1 cup butter

½ cup skim milk, divided

2 eggs

1 tablespoon vanilla extract

2 vanilla beans, scraped (or 2 additional tablespoons vanilla extract)

HOW TO MAKE IT

1 Preheat the oven to 350°F and line a cupcake pan with cupcake liners. **2** In a medium bowl, mix together the sugar, flour, baking powder, and salt. **3** Combine the dry ingredients and the butter in the bowl of a standing mixer and mix on low speed until the butter is completely mixed in and there is a mealy consistency. **4** Add ¼ cup of the milk and mix slowly to make a paste. This will break up any lumps that are trying to form. **5** In a separate medium bowl, combine the eggs with the rest of the milk, the vanilla extract, and the vanilla bean scrapings, and slowly pour the mixture into the batter in the standing mixer. Scrape down the sides of the bowl and mix on high for about 10 seconds. **6** With an ice cream scoop, fill the cups in the cupcake pan about ¾ full and bake for 10 to 15 minutes. The cupcake tops will just be slightly golden. If you overbake the cupcakes, brush the tops with Simple Syrup (page 44) right when they come out of the oven and they'll be good to eat that day, but cannot be eaten the next.

YIELD: 12 cupcakes

KEEPS: Three days in the fridge in an airtight container

SIMPLE VEGAN VANILLA CUPCAKES

I was vegan for about eight years, and during this time I had a lot of vegan cupcake mishaps. Some mishaps became awesome recipes, and this is one of them. I cannot stress how important it is to not overmix this batter. Similar to overmixed mashed potatoes, the batter will become like glue and will bake very tough. Just be careful—you've been warned. Use this recipe in place of Vanilla Bean Cupcakes anywhere in this book.

⅓ cup palm shortening (vegan margarine is OK, too, but adds too much salt even if you take the salt out of the recipe)

1 cup sugar

1⅓ cups all-purpose flour, sifted

1 tablespoon baking powder

1 tablespoon salt

3¼ cups vegan milk (soy, rice, hemp, or almond)

1 tablespoon vanilla extract

1 tablespoon vanilla bean paste or the scrapings from 2 vanilla beans

HOW TO MAKE IT

1 Preheat the oven to 325°F and line a cupcake pan with cupcake liners. **2** In a standing mixer with the paddle attachment, cream the shortening with the sugar on medium speed until it's light and fluffy. **3** In a medium bowl, mix together the flour, baking powder, and salt. **4** In a separate bowl, mix together the milk, the vanilla extract, and the vanilla bean paste or scrapings. **5** Slowly alternate adding the dry ingredients and the milk mixture to the standing mixer, scraping down the sides of the bowl each time. Mix until just incorporated; do not mix any more than absolutely necessary. **6** With the ice cream scoop, fill the cups in the cupcake pan about ¾ full and bake for about 20 minutes. The middles of the cupcakes will be spongy, but may not spring back when touched.

YIELD: 12 cupcakes

KEEPS: Cannot be stored, must be used at once (really, don't store this one)

Devil's Food Cupcakes

This vegan chocolate cupcake is hands down the very best recipe we've ever made. It's vegan but doesn't scream vegan. We've done many taste tests with this cupcake up against a non-vegan competitor and it won every single time. We now use it for almost every chocolate cake concoction we make.

1⅓ cups all-purpose flour

1⅓ cups sugar

½ cup cocoa powder

1 tablespoon baking soda

2 teaspoons salt

⅓ cup canola or sunflower oil

1 tablespoon vinegar

1 tablespoon vanilla

1 cup hot coffee

HOW TO MAKE IT

1 Preheat the oven to 350°F and line a cupcake pan with cupcake liners. **2** Place the flour, sugar, cocoa powder, baking soda, and salt in a large bowl and mix together with a whisk. **3** In a small bowl, combine the oil, vinegar, and vanilla. Slowly pour this mixture into the mixing bowl while whisking, and then continue whisking as you slowly pour in the hot coffee. **4** At this point there'll be some lumps—it'll happen, so don't think you screwed up. There are two things you can do: You can try to whisk them out, or you can clean your hands and get them out with your fingers. This second way may be a little messy, but it beats standing there endlessly whisking and whisking. **5** With an ice cream scoop, fill the cups in the cupcake pan about ¾ full and bake for about 15 minutes. You're looking for a dime-sized soft, shiny spot in the center of the cupcakes that looks like it's not all the way cooked; this is when you know they're done.

YIELD: 12 cupcakes

KEEPS: Up to five days in the fridge, tightly covered

ALTERNATIVE-SUGAR DEVIL'S FOOD CUPCAKES

This is a sugar-alternative, vegan devil's food like no other. The number of requests we receive for so many different allergy-friendly cupcakes is truly mind-blowing. After years of saying no, I gave in and started to play with alternative sweeteners. I've found a few that work great and are chemical free. This recipe uses blue agave syrup and is my favorite so far.

2 tablespoons hot water

2 tablespoons freeze-dried espresso

1¹/₃ cups all-purpose flour

½ cup cocoa powder

1 tablespoon baking soda

2 teaspoons salt

¹/₃ cup canola or sunflower oil

1 teaspoon vinegar

1 tablespoon vanilla

1¹/₃ cups agave syrup

HOW TO MAKE IT

1 Preheat the oven to 350°F and line a cupcake pan with cupcake liners. **2** In a small bowl, mix the hot water and freeze-dried espresso together and set aside. **3** Place the flour, cocoa powder, baking soda, and salt in a large bowl and mix them together with a whisk. **4** In a separate medium bowl, combine the oil, vinegar, vanilla, and agave. **5** Pour the agave mixture into the dry ingredients while slowly whisking, and then add the hot-water-and-espresso concoction. At this point there'll be some lumps, so don't think you screwed up. There are two things you can do: You can try to whisk them out, or you can clean your hands and get them out with your fingers. This second solution may be a little messy, but it beats standing there endlessly whisking. **6** With an ice cream scoop, fill each cup in the cupcake pan about ¾ full and bake for about 15 minutes. You're looking for a dime-sized soft, shiny spot in the center of the cupcakes that looks like it's not cooked all the way; this is when you know they're done.

YIELD: 12 cupcakes

KEEPS: Up to five days in the fridge, tightly covered

CHOCOLATE SPONGE CUPCAKES

This is a French-style cupcake (if that's not an oxymoron), and the recipe is a bit complicated but makes a really good base for unique cupcakes when you really want the filling and frosting to be the stars.

1 cup all-purpose flour, sifted

1 cup cocoa powder, extra brute (good-quality, dark, without sugar added)

20 egg yolks

2½ cups sugar, divided

20 egg whites

HOW TO MAKE IT

1 Preheat the oven to 350°F and line a cupcake pan with cupcake liners. **2** Sift together the flour and cocoa powder into a small bowl and set aside. **3** Whisk the egg yolks on high speed in a standing mixer while pouring in 1¼ cups of the sugar. Whisk until the mixture is lightened to a butter color, about 8 to 10 minutes, then pour it into a separate mixing bowl and set aside. **4** Clean the bowl of the standing mixer really well; make sure there is no yolk left, or the egg whites will not rise at all. **5** With the clean bowl on the standing mixer, whip the egg whites on a slow speed for a few minutes (but no more than 5 minutes, or you'll add air to the whites). This breaks up the proteins, warms them up a little, and helps the cupcakes rise. **6** Turn the mixer on high and slowly add the remaining sugar. Whip until soft peaks form, about 8 minutes. Soft peaks are a little droopy, so you want light, airy whites that don't hold their shape well. **7** Take a little bit of the yolks that were set aside and fold them into the whites with a rubber spatula (this is called tempering). Then dump this all into the yolks and slowly fold them together—do not overmix the ingredients or handle them roughly. **8** When the mixture is almost combined, delicately fold in the flour and cocoa powder. **9** Once the batter is combined, use an ice cream scoop to fill the cups in the cupcake pan about ¾ full and bake for about 10 minutes. When a toothpick comes out clean, you're cool to take them out of the oven.

YIELD: 12 cupcakes

KEEPS: Must be used right away, cannot be stored at all

LeMON CUPCAKES

I've tried many lemon cakes in my day because lemon is one of my favorite flavors. This French-style cake always stood out as the very best because it uses eggs as the leavener, which adds to the lean lemon flavor. These cupcakes dry out quickly, so you'll need to use them as soon as they're baked.

2 cups (1 pound) butter

8 eggs

2 cups sugar

8 cups flour

½ cup lemon zest

HOW TO MAKE IT

1 Preheat the oven to 325°F and line a cupcake pan with cupcake liners. **2** Place butter in a microwave-safe bowl and heat it for a few seconds on high power, then mix it with a rubber spatula and microwave it a little more. Continue to do this until the butter has a mayo consistency but is not totally melted to a liquid. **3** Place the eggs in the bowl of a standing mixer with a whip attachment and slowly whip them at low speed. **4** Slowly pour in the sugar and bring the mixer up to high speed. **5** Whip the eggs with the sugar until a light butter color is achieved and the mixture comes up to the top of the bowl while it's whipping. **6** Turn the mixer down to low speed and add in the flour. Mix just until incorporated. **7** Take the mixer bowl off of the mixer and fold in the butter and the lemon zest by hand with a rubber spatula. **8** With an ice cream scoop, fill the cups in the cupcake pan about ¾ full and bake for about 15 minutes. The cupcakes will not get a lot of color; they'll just turn golden.

YIELD: 12 cupcakes

KEEPS: Must be used right away

Italian Buttercream

I love Italian buttercream. For me, it's the paragon of what frosting should taste like, but I know it's not for everyone. It's much less sweet and way more buttery than traditional grocery-store frostings. When used improperly or eaten too cold, it tastes just like butter, so temperature is key. It colors well, but will change the color slightly since the butter creates a yellow base. Also, it's very easy to flavor with oils or superconcentrated purées.

¼ cup hot water

1 cup sugar

12 egg whites (fresh, with no yolk, not even the littlest bit)

2 pounds butter, cubed and soft

2 tablespoons vanilla extract

HOW TO MAKE IT

1 Pour the water and then the sugar into a very clean soup pot (any food remnants will cause the sugar to crystallize) and put it on high heat. You want to cook this sugar quickly so it won't have time to crystallize. It's human nature to want to stir this, but don't—just leave it alone. Sugar does not like to be interrupted. **2** While the sugar is cooking, pour the egg whites into the bowl of the standing mixer and whisk on medium speed to break up the proteins and warm up the whites, about 5 minutes. **3** Go back to the sugar. When it first starts to boil, the bubbles will be little and fast, and when it is done the bubbles will be slow and big. This happens quickly. Traditionally, you're taught to use a thermometer when boiling sugar, but I don't trust them—I trust my eyes. The stage you're looking for is called "soft ball." Once the sugar comes to a slow boil, turn off the heat. **4** Whip the egg whites on high speed until soft peaks form, turn the mixer back to medium speed, and slowly pour the hot sugar carefully into the egg whites. Aim for the small space in between the bowl and the whisk; this way you won't end up with clumps of sugar in your buttercream. **5** Once the sugar is incorporated, turn the mixer back to high speed and start incorporating cubes of butter one at a time (otherwise they'll fly back out at you). **6** Once all the butter is incorporated, let the buttercream mix for about 10 minutes or until it's white in color and very light and fluffy. Then add the vanilla extract.

NOTE: When using this buttercream right out of the fridge, you'll need to microwave it for about 30 seconds at a time until it becomes soft again. Then you'll need to re-whip it to be sure the consistency is right.

YIELD: 6 cups, or enough for about 12 cupcakes

KEEPS: In an airtight container for about three days at a cool room temperature, or for about a week in the fridge

American Buttercream

The pastry geek inside of me does not want to call this recipe buttercream, but I've learned that it's what most people think of when they ask for buttercream, so I gave in. I named it American Buttercream because when I worked in Europe, it was unheard of and just considered an American thing. We keep this recipe vegan because it stores better and longer, and vegan margarine has a good salt content. You can always equally substitute milk and butter for the vegan components, but you'll have to use the buttercream right away and not store it, as it will sour.

1 cup shortening (I prefer palm)

½ cup vegan margarine

4 cups powdered sugar, sifted

¼ cup soymilk

2 tablespoons vanilla extract

HOW TO MAKE IT VANILLA

1 Combine the shortening and margarine in the bowl of a standing mixer and mix on high until all lumps are out and the consistency is light and fluffy. **2** While the mixer is on low, slowly add the powdered sugar then the vanilla, and then the soymilk at the end. **3** Scrape down the sides of the bowl and put the mixer on high for about 10 minutes, the longer the better—your goal is to mix out any of the graininess from the powdered sugar.

HOW TO MAKE IT CHOCOLATE

1 Substitute ½ cup of extra-brute (no sugar added) cocoa powder for ½ cup powdered sugar. If the consistency gets too thick, add an extra touch of soymilk.

NOTE: This frosting can be colored and flavored with many different components. Each cupcake recipe calls for something different to be done to the buttercream to kind of break up that sugar high that you usually achieve with this type of frosting.

YIELD: 6 cups, or enough for about 12 cupcakes

KEEPS: About a week at room temperature, but does not store well in the fridge

CrEAM CHEeSE FROStiNG

Cream cheese frosting is my favorite. It has the most personality, and it goes well with so many flavors. White chocolate (which I usually do not care for) and lemon zest make our version unique and a little extra special. This frosting does not color well—the colors break down the proteins and make it slimy—just keep this one natural, but use it in a fun and decorative way.

¼ cup white chocolate pieces

½ cup soft butter (leave it on your counter overnight)

4 cups powdered sugar, sifted

1 cup cold cream cheese (right out of the fridge)

2 tablespoons lemon zest

HOW TO MAKE IT

1 Melt the white chocolate pieces in the microwave for 10 second intervals on high power, stirring in between. **2** In a standing mixer, mix the butter with the powdered sugar on medium speed until both are light and soft and there are no lumps, about 8 minutes, then scrape down the sides of the bowl. **3** With the mixer on low, slowly add the cream cheese in chunks (I just pull it off the block by hand). **4** Once it's all in there, scrape down the sides of the bowl, turn the mixer on high, and pour in the white chocolate and lemon zest; let the mixer run for about 8 more minutes. The frosting should be lump-free, airy, and white in color.

HOW TO MAKE IT VEGAN

1 Substitute Earth Balance or another vegan margarine for the butter and substitute Tofutti vegan cream cheese for the regular cream cheese. Take out the white chocolate and add 1 tablespoon vanilla. **2** Follow the directions for the non-vegan frosting. It'll be a little looser than the regular frosting, but just as delicious.

NOTE: If you were to store this in the fridge for later use, to get the consistency back you'll need to either mix it again in the standing mixer for 4 to 5 minutes on medium speed or microwave it for 15 seconds on high and then stir it.

YIELD: 6 cups, or enough for about 12 cupcakes

KEEPS: About a week in the fridge in an airtight container

GaNaCHE

Ganache is one of those basic things that I think everyone should know how to make. It's an excellent filling and frosting when used at different temperatures. It pleases a palette that doesn't like "sweet" very much and also can be transformed into so many different flavors. This recipe is very easy to manipulate—if you'd rather have a softer or harder product, you can just adjust the amount of cream.

3 cups dark chocolate

4 tablespoons butter

2 tablespoons honey or agave syrup

1 cup heavy cream

HOW TO MAKE IT

1 *Start the day before*—Place chocolate, butter, and honey or agave in a mixing bowl. **2** Heat the cream in a soup pot over medium heat, stirring constantly, until the cream comes to a boil. Then pour the cream over the chocolate and honey or agave and let sit for about 5 minutes. **3** Whisk the ingredients together. The mixture will be liquidy, but don't be scared—it'll set up. **4** Cover the bowl with plastic wrap so that the plastic is actually touching the surface of the ganache, and let it sit overnight at a cool room temperature. **5** After the ganache has sat overnight, it can be used as frosting as is. If you'd like an airier, lighter frosting, you can whip it in a standing mixer, but it'll make the ganache dull-looking and a little broken. To use it as a filling, just microwave it for a few seconds to get to a syrupy consistency and pour it into the center of cupcakes with holes poked through them.

NOTE: Many of my cupcake recipes call for this ganache recipe to be flavored, and it's very easy to do. As long as you keep the same quantities of liquid and solid ingredients, you're golden. For instance, if you'd like a whiskey ganache (like in Love Kills, page 63), replace half the cream with whiskey. The trick is that you won't want to heat up the whiskey, so you'll need to melt the chocolate first and add the whiskey after the cream has been mixed in.

NOTE: How to fix a broken ganache—A broken ganache looks like a vinaigrette before you mix it: The fat separates from the mixture and makes streaks in the chocolate and gives it a grainy texture. To fix it, heat up the ganache in a saucepan over medium heat until it's hot enough to make it all spreadable, then transfer it to a mixing bowl. In a separate pan, heat up a little bit of heavy cream and pour it into the middle of the broken ganache. Slowly whisk it in, starting from the middle, making your way to the side of the bowl. Stop whisking when the ganache has become smooth and silky looking.

YIELD: About 4 cups

KEEPS: Two days at room temperature if sealed with plastic wrap (the plastic wrap should be touching the ganache so no air gets in), or up to five days in the fridge sealed with plastic wrap

FrENCH MErINGUE

French meringue is the purest of the classic meringues and emulates marshmallow well and acts as a light frosting. It's very important that you do not make the meringue in advance because it won't hold up for long. Make what you need right when you need it.

6 egg whites (make sure there are *no yolks*)
1 cup sugar

HOW TO MAKE IT

1 Place the egg whites and the sugar in the bowl of a standing mixer and heat the ingredients together over a double boiler. **2** Whisk the ingredients together until the sugar is somewhat dissolved and the mixture is warm to the touch, about 2 or 3 minutes. Make sure to keep the ingredients moving because you aren't trying to cook anything—you just want to warm the ingredients and make them be better friends. **3** Once the mixture is heated, place the bowl back onto the standing mixer and whip the ingredients on high for about 10 minutes. You don't need to whip until it's cool (a myth), but you want to stop whipping when the peaks are glossy and can hold their shape. If the mixture looks grainy, you went too far, and the meringue will break down on the cupcakes.

YIELD: 6 cups, or enough for 12 cupcakes
KEEPS: Does not keep

ALL-PURPOSE CARAMEL

Everyone needs a good caramel recipe. I have a firm belief that good caramel is a bit dark and always salted. If that's not your preference, I forgive you; this recipe can be made lighter, and you can easily omit the salt if you'd like. The cool thing about this caramel is that it can be used as a filling, mixed into frosting, and, if you need some coffee while you're baking (as I do), it tastes great in coffee drinks!

4 cups sugar	2 tablespoons unsalted butter
¼ teaspoon fleur de sel or sea salt	3 cups heavy cream

HOW TO MAKE IT

1 Put the sugar in a very clean, hard-bottomed soup pot (if your pot isn't clean, the sugar will crystallize and you'll have chunky caramel) over medium heat. It's human nature to want to touch and play with things, but try really hard to restrain yourself. Only stir this sugar once, with a wooden spoon, to make sure it's browning evenly. Then leave it alone. **2** Allow the caramel to cook for about 15 to 20 minutes, until it reaches your desired color—the longer you cook it, the darker and more bitter it'll get. **3** Once the sugar is colored evenly and completely melted, take it off the heat and stir in the salt and butter until melted. **4** Microwave the cream to a warm room temperature for about 2 minutes on high power and slowly pour it into the sugar while whisking. BE CAREFUL! Caramel bites back. It'll heat the cream very fast and a very hot steam will come off the top. Wear oven mitts or have superfast reflexes. **5** Cool the caramel in the pot—it will melt anything else.

NOTE: If you refrigerate the caramel, just microwave it on high power in 1-minute intervals, stirring between each heating, to bring it back to a workable consistency.

YIELD: 4 cups

KEEPS: In an airtight container for 24 hours at room temperature, or a week in the fridge

CHOCOLATE CIGARETTES

Chocolate work always seems scary to people, but it doesn't have to. These decorations are quick and fun and can accent any cupcake or cake. Just remember that temperature is everything.

2 pounds dark chocolate with a high cocoa
content (72% is perfect), divided

HOW TO MAKE IT

1 To temper the chocolate, ensuring that it'll be shiny and hold its shape, slowly melt 1 pound of the chocolate in a microwave-safe bowl in the microwave on high for 30 seconds at a time. **2** Once it's all melted, start stirring in cool chocolate pieces to slowly bring the temperature down so the chocolate is in a cool liquid state. This is called seeding. The easiest way to see if your chocolate is tempered is to put a little bit on the middle of your bottom lip. Once it feels cool, it's ready. **3** On a marble slab, drizzle several lines of chocolate about 12 inches long and spread them thinly with an offset spatula so they're about 3 inches wide. Wait for the chocolate to cool, but don't wait until it's so cool that it has completely hardened to the marble. **4** Using a metal bench scraper or a palette knife, start quickly making your cigarettes. Place the scraper about an inch from the edge of the chocolate and quickly push sideways so the chocolate rolls into cigarette shapes. **5** Repeat steps 3 and 4 until you have enough cigarettes for your cupcakes.

HOW TO MAKE IT CHOCOLATE CURLS

1 Temper the chocolate like you would to make Chocolate Cigarettes, according to steps 1 and 2, above.
2 Instead of drizzling the tempered chocolate on a marble slab, as above, pour the chocolate onto the back of a clean cookie sheet and spread it in a thin layer with an offset spatula. **3** When the chocolate starts to cool, but is still a bit malleable, hold a circular cookie cutter at a 45-degree angle and drag it along the cookie sheet to make big curls, about 1½ inches wide. You'll need to do this fast or you'll have to re-seed your chocolate.

YIELD: 12 cigarettes

KEEPS: Uncovered at room temperature, or in a plastic container in the freezer, but not in the fridge, or they'll condensate

CHOCOLATE SAUCE

Like most basic recipes, this chocolate sauce is multipurpose. Not only can you use it in some pretty amazing cupcakes, you can also use it in mochas and hot chocolates.

2 cups cocoa powder, extra brute (no sugar added, please)

1¼ cups water

2 tablespoons agave syrup

HOW TO MAKE IT

1 Place the cocoa powder, water, and agave syrup in a medium-sized, heavy-duty saucepan over medium-high heat and whisk while bringing the mixture to a boil. Let it boil for about 2 minutes. **2** Transfer the sauce to a heat-safe storage container and allow it to cool.

YIELD: About 3 cups

KEEPS: About five days in the fridge

Lemon Curd

Fruit curd is a kitchen, or at least a baking, staple. A good recipe can yield many different flavored curds using the same ratio of ingredients. This one has always worked for me—hopefully it will for you. Curd can be used for many things, including like jam on toast!

1¾ cups sugar	4 eggs
1 cup lemon juice	1 cup butter, cut into 1-inch cubes
¼ cup lemon zest	

HOW TO MAKE IT

1 Fill a large saucepan with several inches of water and bring the water to a boil. Set a metal bowl on top of the pot to make a double boiler. **2** Combine the sugar and the lemon juice in the bowl and stir until well-mixed, then add the lemon zest and the eggs last. Stir the mixture constantly so the raw sugar doesn't touch the yolks for any period of time—sugar cooks yolks and you'll end up with little pieces of overcooked egg that are pretty hard to strain out. **3** Cook the mixture over the double boiler, stirring often, until it becomes the consistency of ketchup. **4** Run the mixture through a strainer into a heatproof container. **5** Stir in the butter and then chill the curd in the refrigerator.

HOW TO MAKE IT MANGO

1 Follow the directions for the lemon curd, but substitute mango purée for the lemon juice and keep in the lemon zest for a little tang.

HOW TO MAKE IT GRAPEFRUIT

1 Follow the directions for the lemon curd, but substitute grapefruit juice for the lemon juice and leave out the lemon zest.

YIELD: About 4 cups

KEEPS: About a week in the fridge in an airtight container

PASTRY CREAM

Pastry cream is incredibly multipurpose. Honestly, the possibilities are endless, such as éclair filling, as a great base for vanilla mousse, and as donut filling.

1 cup whole milk	4 egg yolks
½ a vanilla bean	1 tablespoon cornstarch
¼ cup sugar	2 tablespoons butter

HOW TO MAKE IT

1 In a medium-sized, thick-bottomed saucepan, place the milk, the vanilla bean scrapings, the vanilla bean pod, and the sugar. **2** In a small bowl, place the egg yolks and the cornstarch and whisk them together. **3** Bring the pot with the milk mixture to a simmer over medium heat. Once it's heated, pour half of it into the egg yolk mixture while whisking. If you don't whisk while pouring the milk, the egg yolks will just cook and you'll have scrambled eggs. A good trick for how to keep the bowl from moving while you're whisking is to wrap a wet dish towel around the base of the bowl. **4** Once half the mixture is poured into the yolks, pour it all back into the pot and slowly bring everything to a boil over medium heat while whisking. **5** Once you see the first few bubbles, pull the pot off the stove, whisk the mixture briskly, and put the pot back onto the heat. Stop cooking when you see bubbles in the middle of the mixture. That means it has come to a complete boil. **6** Toss in the butter and stir until it's melted. **7** Place the cream in a heatproof container and cover immediately with plastic wrap. Leave the cream to cool for about 15 minutes before you put it in the refrigerator or you'll heat up your fridge too much.

YIELD: About 2½ cups

KEEPS: About three days covered in the fridge

MARSHMALLOW

This marshmallow recipe doesn't work well to just munch on—the flavor isn't deep enough— but for the purposes of this book, it's perfect and easy enough to make at home.

2 cups cold water, divided

2 cups sugar

2 (½-tablespoon) packages powdered gelatin (see note)

1 cup powdered sugar

1 cup cornstarch

HOW TO MAKE IT

1 *Start the day before*—Place 1 cup of water in a super-clean, medium-sized, thick-bottomed saucepan and then add the sugar. Make sure the sugar goes right onto the water, not onto the sides of the pot. Put the pot over medium heat. **2** In the bowl of a standing mixer with the wire whip attachment, pour the remaining cup of water and both packets of gelatin, then let the mixture sit for about 5 minutes. **3** On the stove, bring the sugar and water to boil. Once it's boiling, give it one stir with a wooden spoon to make sure there are no sugar granules stuck to the bottom, and let it boil for an additional 2 minutes. **4** Turn the mixer on low and slowly pour the sugar mixture in with the gelatin mixture (be careful, hot sugar hurts). Once it's completely mixed in, turn the mixer on high. **5** Once the mixture becomes stiff (the peaks won't be stiff, but you'll hear the mixer slow down), spray a rubber spatula with spray oil and scrape out the marshmallow on to an 8 x 8-inch baking dish sprayed with spray oil and lined with spray-oiled plastic wrap. **6** Mix the powdered sugar and cornstarch together in a small bowl. Once the marshmallow has cooled, cut it into squares, and dust the top with the powdered sugar mixture. This takes the stickiness away. **7** Let it sit out overnight (but no more than 8 hours) to develop a crust on top. Once the crust has developed, spray it with spray oil and cover it with the plastic.

NOTE: Knox is my preferred brand of gelatin. If you want to keep these vegetarian, you can use agar agar and carrageenan.

YIELD: 64 (1-inch) marshmallows

KEEPS: About a week at room temperature, or in the fridge for three weeks

FONCER DOUGH

In my personal opinion, this is the most important recipe in this book. Seriously, you can use it for everything from quiche to pie dough, and it's super easy to make. Wow, you're lucky!

¾ cup water

½ cup sugar

2 teaspoons salt

¾ pound butter, cut into 1-inch pieces

1 pound pastry flour

6 egg yolks

HOW TO MAKE IT

1 *Start the day before*—In the bowl of a standing mixer with a dough hook attachment, place the sugar and water and stir until the sugar dissolves. Then add the salt. **2** Add the butter and start the mixer on low (with the dough hook). **3** Slowly add the pastry flour and, once the butter and flour are fully incorporated, add the egg yolks. It's important to stop mixing once the egg yolks are incorporated. Mixing too long will make the gluten too strong and will shorten the dough. **4** Shape the dough into a ball and flatten it into a disc. Wrap it with plastic and chill it overnight.

YIELD: About 2 pounds

KEEPS: About three weeks wrapped in plastic in the freezer

SiMPLE SYrUP

Simple syrup has a lot of applications. In this book it's mainly used to add shots of flavor to cupcakes, so my syrup recipe is rather thin. However, you can double the sugar to make a thicker sorbet or popsicle base and many other things. I strongly suggest making a big batch of this so you'll always have some on hand.

1 cup water
1 cup sugar

HOW TO MAKE IT

1 Place the sugar and water in a small saucepan and bring to a simmer. **2** Make sure all the sugar is dissolved in the water, and you're done!

YIELD: 2 cups

KEEPS: About a week covered at room temperature, or about a month covered in the fridge

HAPPY HOuR

*****

MOJITO

I have a newfound love for mojitos. At a vegan restaurant in San Francisco, I was served one with the addition of ginger and blackberries, and I couldn't believe I had not included the mojito in my life sooner. This cupcake only uses the ginger, but if you'd like to add blackberries, no one's stopping you.

Cupcakes
1 recipe Vanilla Bean Cupcakes (page 16)

¼ cup grated fresh ginger

½ cup fresh mint

2 vanilla beans, scraped

1 recipe Simple Syrup (page 44)

1 cup rum

Frosting
1 recipe Vanilla American Buttercream (page 27)

¼ cup rum

2 tablespoons fresh mint, finely shredded

Candied Mint Garnish
12 large whole fresh mint leaves

1 egg white

½ cup sugar, for sprinkling (you might not need all of it)

HOW TO MAKE IT

Candied Mint Garnish **1** *Start the day before*—Brush the mint leaves with the egg white and sprinkle them with sugar, then set them aside to dry. This is a quick way to candy herbs.

Cupcakes **1** Prepare the Vanilla Bean Cupcake batter according to the recipe directions. **2** Add the grated ginger, mint, and the scrapings from the vanilla beans to the batter and bake according to the recipe directions. **3** Mix the rum into the simple syrup. **4** As soon as the cupcakes are out of the oven, brush the tops with the simple syrup. Make sure they're still hot so the flavor of the syrup really penetrates the cupcake. Allow the cupcakes to cool before frosting.

Frosting **1** Prepare the Vanilla American Buttercream according to the recipe directions. **2** Add the rum and mint to the buttercream with a whisk.

Put It All Together **1** Frost the cooled cupcakes with the minted frosting using a piping bag with a star tip. **2** Top each one with a candied mint leaf and candied ginger, if you have it.

TEQUILA AND LIME

This cupcake is pretty self-explanatory. Tequila and lime is such a perfect combination, there's no need to substitute anything.

Cupcakes
1 recipe Vanilla Bean Cupcakes (page 16)

1 cup fresh lime zest

juice of 4 limes

1 cup tequila

Frosting
1 recipe Vanilla American Buttercream (page 27)

2 tablespoons lime juice

HOW TO MAKE IT

Cupcakes **1** Prepare the Vanilla Bean Cupcake batter according to the recipe directions, and add the lime zest with the wet ingredients. **2** Bake the cupcakes according to the recipe directions. **3** Mix the lime juice with the tequila. **4** When the cupcakes come out of the oven, heavily drench them with the tequila-lime mixture.

Frosting **1** Omit the vanilla from the Vanilla American Buttercream. Instead, replace it with the lime juice and mix the buttercream according to the recipe directions.

Put It All Together **1** Using a piping bag with a star tip, frost the cupcakes with the lime frosting. **2** Top each cupcake with a sprinkling of salt and a fresh lime wedge.

SaNGRiA

A few years ago, I thought it would be funny to make a line of cupcakes for Mother's Day that were all inspired by wine and mixed drinks. The Sangria was the most popular and customers continue to order it for weddings and parties.

Cupcakes
1 recipe Vanilla Bean Cupcakes (page 16)

1 cup small-diced fresh Granny Smith apples

1 cup green grapes, sliced in half

4 tablespoons orange zest

1 cup red wine

Apple Chip Garnish
1 recipe Simple Syrup (page 44)

2 apples (Rome or Honey Crisp are best)

lime juice

Frosting
3 cups red wine

1 recipe Vanilla American Buttercream (page 27)

HOW TO MAKE IT

Apple Chip Garnish **1** Preheat the oven to 200°F. **2** Using a mandolin, or your super slicing skills, make thin, large rounds of sliced apple. Brush both sides of the slices with the cool simple syrup and a little bit of lime juice to stop the browning. **3** Place the slices on a Silpat or a baking sheet lined with parchment paper and put in the oven. **4** After about an hour, flip the slices over and leave them in the oven for one more hour. The result should be a paper-thin slice of apple with the color preserved.

Cupcakes **1** Prepare the Vanilla Bean Cupcake batter according to the recipe directions. **2** Fold the apples, grapes, and orange zest into the batter. **3** Bake the cupcakes according to the recipe directions. **4** As soon as they come out of the oven, let a little red wine soak into the tops of the cupcakes with a pastry brush. It's good to do this when the cupcakes are warm because the pores are more open on the tops and will soak up the flavor better.

Red Wine Frosting **1** In a saucepan over medium-high heat, bring the red wine to a boil and allow it to reduce to one cup, making a red wine syrup. **2** Chill this syrup in the refrigerator. **3** Prepare the Vanilla American Buttercream according to the recipe directions. **4** Mix the red wine syrup into the buttercream.

Put It All Together **1** Using a piping bag with a star tip, frost the cupcakes with the buttercream.
2 Top each cupcake with an apple chip pointing straight up. If you have a few extra grapes, you can add those as well.

NOTE: If you find oranges (or any citrus) cheaply in large quantities, you can buy them for the zest and freeze it in an airtight container. Then you don't have to zest every time you want to add a little to your cupcakes or anything else you may need it for.

Irish Car Bomb

This is our answer to a St. Patrick's Day cupcake. However, we've been asked to make it at weddings throughout the entire year, so don't feel like March 17th is the only time it's appropriate.

Cupcakes
1 recipe Chocolate Sponge Cupcakes
(page 22)

Ganache
1 recipe Ganache (page 30)

½ cup whiskey

Frosting
1 recipe Chocolate American Buttercream
(page 27)

1 cup Irish cream

Put It All Together
1 recipe Simple Syrup (page 44)

1 cup whiskey

HOW TO MAKE IT

Ganache **1** *Start the day before*—Prepare the ganache according to the recipe directions, but only use ½ cup cream. **2** Add the heated cream to the chocolate, then stir in the whiskey. **3** Let the ganache set up overnight according to the recipe directions.

Cupcakes **1** Prepare and bake the Chocolate Sponge Cupcakes according to the recipe directions.

Frosting **1** Prepare the Chocolate American Buttercream according to the recipe directions, and when it's almost whipped together, slowly add the Irish cream and whip it until it's combined.

Put It All Together **1** Add the whiskey to the simple syrup. **2** Heavily soak the cooled cupcakes with the syrup. **3** With your index finger, poke a hole in each cupcake and fill them with the whiskey ganache. **4** Chill the cupcakes for about 5 minutes in the fridge and then dip their tops into the remaining whiskey ganache. **5** Using a piping bag with a star tip, swirl on the Irish cream buttercream. I top these cupcakes with a little atom bomb made out of fondant, but they could also get a drizzle of ganache or even melted chocolate.

STRAWBERRY DAIQUIRI

I designed this cupcake for a Hawaiian-themed party, and even though I'm not a coconut fan, it turned out better than I ever expected. I also though the finished look was really cute, which is part of the reason they became a shop staple the whole summer.

Cupcakes

1 cup butter, softened

2 cups sugar

3 cups flour

2 teaspoons salt

2 teaspoons baking powder

1 cup coconut milk

1 cup coconut cream

6 egg whites (no little yolk bits), at room temperature

2 tablespoons triple sec

1 cup rum

½ cup lime juice

1 recipe Simple Syrup (page 44)

Put It All Together

2 cups strawberry jam or compote

Frosting

1 recipe Vanilla American Buttercream (page 27)

¼ cup coconut milk (canned is fine, but fresh is best)

12 White Chocolate Cigarettes (page 37)

HOW TO MAKE IT

Cupcakes **1** Preheat the oven to 350°F and line the cupcake pan with cupcake liners. **2** In a standing mixer with the paddle attachment, mix the butter and sugar together until light and fluffy, about 10 to 15 minutes, then scrape down the sides of the bowl. **3** In a medium bowl, mix the flour, salt, and baking powder together. In a separate medium bowl, mix the coconut milk and coconut cream together. **4** Slowly alternate adding the dry ingredients with the coconut liquids to the standing mixer. Stop a few times to scrape down the sides of the bowl. Once all the ingredients have been placed in the bowl, turn the mixer on high for just a few seconds to wake up the batter a little, but not so much as to overmix it. **5** Set the batter aside in the large mixing bowl and wash the bowl from the standing mixer well (fat breaks down egg whites—they really hate each other—so if any butter fat is left in the bowl, the next step won't work). **6** In the standing mixer with the whip attachment, whisk the egg whites until soft peaks form, about 5 minutes. Egg whites really like to whip when they are at least at room temperature, if not warmer, and the colder they are the longer they will take to whip. If you're in a hurry, you can always warm them in a bowl over simmering water while keeping them moving with a spatula. If you choose this method, you have to stand there and actually pay attention to them or you will end up with a bowl of cooked egg whites. Soft peaks should form fast under the right conditions. If you are scared, whipping them too little is fine, but overwhipped egg whites won't work well. So when in doubt, slightly underwhip. You'll get better at it, I promise. **7** Once you have the egg whites whipped and the batter made, slowly fold the whites into the batter, a little bit at the time, with a rubber spatula. Don't go crazy with this. If you deflate the egg whites, they won't help give the cupcakes structure and they will sink in the middle. **8** Scoop the batter into the cupcake pan with the ice cream scoop, filling the cups in the cupcake pan about ¾ full and bake for about 15 minutes or until a toothpick comes out clean. **9** While the cupcakes are baking, add the triple sec, rum, and lime juice to cooled simple syrup. **10** When the cupcakes come out of the oven, immediately soak them with the simple syrup and use your index finger to poke holes through the centers.

Frosting **1** Prepare the Vanilla American Buttercream according to the recipe directions, but omit the soymilk and replace it with the coconut milk.

Put It All Together **1** Fill the cooled cupcakes with your favorite strawberry jam or compote. **2** Frost each one with a large dollop of the coconut buttercream, and top them with white chocolate cigarettes for straws and paper umbrellas!

BLOODY MARY

Who needs a drink at brunch when you can have a cupcake?

Cupcakes
1 recipe Vanilla Bean Cupcakes (page 16)

2 cups cherry tomatoes

1 tablespoon coarsely ground black pepper

1½ cups vodka

Celery Garnish
3 or 4 celery stalks

1 recipe Simple Syrup (page 44)

Frosting
1 recipe Vanilla American Buttercream (page 27)

¼ cup Tabasco sauce

HOW TO MAKE IT

Cupcakes **1** Omit the vanilla extract and vanilla bean scrapings from the Vanilla Bean Cupcake batter. Otherwise, prepare the batter according to the recipe directions. **2** Cut the cherry tomatoes in half. Fold them into the cupcake batter with the black pepper. **3** Bake the cupcakes according to the recipe directions. **4** When the cupcakes come out of the oven, heavily drench them with the vodka.

Celery Garnish **1** Cut the celery stalks into 2-inch pieces and blanch them really quickly in rapidly boiling water for about 1 minute. **2** Strain the celery and add the pieces to the simple syrup. **3** Bring the syrup to a boil for about a minute and then turn the flame off. Let the celery cool and then bring it to a boil again for another minute. Repeat this process two or three times until the celery is translucent.

Frosting **1** Omit the vanilla extract from the Vanilla American Buttercream recipe. **2** Fold the Tabasco sauce into the finished buttercream.

Put It All Together **1** Using a piping bag with a star tip, frost the cupcakes. **2** Top each cupcake with a few pieces of candied celery. You can also sprinkle a little cracked black pepper on top.

TEQUILA SUNRISE

In general, I find mixed drinks very inspiring. I use them in a lot of my creations, cupcakes and beyond. I was given a bottle of tequila by a friend whose family distills it in Mexico, and out came this cupcake.

Cupcakes
1 recipe Vanilla Bean Cupcakes (page 16)
1 cup tequila, divided
4 tablespoons orange zest
1 recipe Simple Syrup (page 44)

Frosting
1 recipe Vanilla American Buttercream (page 27)
1 cup powdered sugar
½ cup tequila
2 tablespoons orange zest

HOW TO MAKE IT

Cupcakes **1** Prepare the Vanilla Bean Cupcake batter according to the recipe directions, but leave out the milk, vanilla extract, and vanilla beans. Instead, replace the milk with ½ cup tequila and then mix the orange zest into the finished batter. **2** Bake the cupcakes according to the recipe directions. **3** Add the remaining ½ cup tequila to the simple syrup. **4** As soon as the cupcakes come out of the oven, drench them with the syrup, then allow them to cool.

Frosting **1** Prepare the Vanilla American Buttercream according to the recipe directions, but leave out the vanilla extract. Make the buttercream extra stiff by adding the extra cup of powdered sugar. **2** Once the frosting is mixed, stir in the tequila and orange zest.

Put It All Together **1** Frost the cooled cupcakes with a piping bag with a star tip. I like to make the frosting look like a flame, so I split it in half and use food coloring to make one half red and one half yellow and put them in the piping bag side by side. The color will come out looking like a flame and will make a very fiery orange color at the end. Usually I put a white chocolate cigarette right in the middle of each cupcake to look like a straw.

Chocolate Cherry Stout

I love beer. I really, really love beer, and I especially love beer when I don't have the guilt of actually drinking it. This cupcake is the perfect combination of beer, fruit, and frosting. It certainly is a winter cupcake and won't taste right in the summer.

Cupcakes

¾ cup stout beer (we like using a chocolate stout, but any stout will do)

¾ cup blackstrap molasses

¼ teaspoon baking soda

1½ cups all-purpose flour

¾ teaspoon baking powder

2 tablespoons ground ginger

¾ teaspoon ground cinnamon

¼ teaspoon ground nutmeg

a pinch of ground cardamom

8 eggs

1½ cups sugar

⅛ cup sunflower oil (you can also get fancy and use toasted hazelnut oil)

2 cups sweet cherries, pitted and chopped (don't use pie cherries—they're too bitter and react badly with the taste of the stout)

1 cup toasted, chopped hazelnuts

Frosting

1 recipe Italian Buttercream (page 24)

Put It All Together

2 tablespoons toasted, chopped hazelnuts, for garnish

HOW TO MAKE IT

Frosting **1** **Start the day before**—Place the butter for the Italian Buttercream in a heavy-bottomed saucepan over high heat. Let the butter melt and start to brown. **2** Let the butter go to a caramel color, then remove it from the heat. Some bits of butter will stick to the bottom of the pan, but don't waste these—they're really tasty. **3** Put the browned butter in the fridge to chill overnight. **4** The next day, follow the directions for making the buttercream, using the browned butter, and mix in the hazelnuts.

Cupcakes **1** *Start the day before*—Bring the stout and molasses to a boil together in a small soup pot. Do not stir the mixture or it will boil over. **2** Once the mixture is boiling, remove the pot from the heat and mix in the baking soda. It will foam up—don't be scared. **3** Let the stout and molasses mixture sit to cool for a few minutes, then transfer it to your fridge and let it chill overnight. **4** The next day, preheat the oven to 350°F and line a cupcake pan with cupcake liners. **5** Place the flour, baking powder, ginger, cinnamon, nutmeg, and cardamom in a mixing bowl and mix together with a whisk. **6** In a small bowl, combine the eggs, sugar, oil, and the molasses and stout mixture. **7** Slowly pour the wet ingredients into the mixing bowl with the dry ingredients and whisk until smooth and silky. This is a very wet batter. **8** Fold the cherries and hazelnuts into the batter. **9** Using an ice cream scoop, fill the cups in the cupcake pan about ¾ full and bake for about 15 minutes. The cupcake tops will rise a lot and become a bit crusty—this is normal.

Put It All Together **1** Using a piping bag with a star tip, lightly frost the cooled cupcakes. I say lightly because the buttercream has a very solid flavor and you don't want it to overpower the cupcake flavor. **2** Top the cupcakes with the toasted, chopped hazelnuts.

LOVE KILLS

I can't stand Valentine's Day, but I am a HUGE Sex Pistols fan. So I made this cupcake for Valentine's Day as a tribute to Sid Vicious in whiskey and chocolate.

Cupcakes
1 recipe Devil's Food Cupcakes (page 19)

1 cup whiskey

1 recipe Simple Syrup (page 44)

Frosting
1 recipe French Meringue (page 32)

Ganache
½ recipe Ganache (page 30)

½ cup whiskey

HOW TO MAKE IT

Cupcakes **1** Prepare and bake the Devil's Food Cupcakes according to the recipe directions. **2** Add the whiskey to the simple syrup. **3** When the cupcakes are hot from the oven, heavily soak them with the syrup.

Ganache **1** *Start the day before*—Use only ½ cup cream. Make the ganache according to the recipe directions. **2** Once the hot cream has been added to the chocolate, stir in the whiskey. **3** Let the ganache set up overnight according to the recipe directions.

Frosting **1** Prepare the French meringue according to the recipe directions.

Put It All Together **1** With your index finger, poke holes through the tops of the cupcakes and fill them with whiskey ganache. **2** In the microwave, melt the ganache left over from filling the cupcakes a little and dip the tops of the cupcakes in it. **3** Put the cupcakes in the fridge for about 5 minutes so the ganache sets up. **4** Using a piping bag with a star tip, put a huge spike of French meringue on top of each cupcake. If you have a crème brûlée torch, use it to toast the meringue. I also usually make a topper for these out of a small picture of Sid glued onto a toothpick.

ROSEWATER CHAMPAGNE

Using floral flavors in baking is tricky. They're really delicious, but when too much or poor-quality extracts are used, you may end up with a "Grandma's bathroom" smell, so BE CAREFUL! Ginger ale is a great nonalcoholic substitute for champagne.

Cupcakes
about 28 rose petals, divided (see note)

1 recipe Vanilla Bean Cupcakes (page 16)

1 tablespoon rose flower water (see note)

1 recipe Simple Syrup (page 44)

Ganache
1 recipe Ganache (page 30)

½ cup champagne (or ginger ale)

HOW TO MAKE IT

Ganache **1** ***Start the day before***—Prepare the ganache according to the recipe directions, but use only ½ cup of cream. **2** Once the cream and the chocolate have been stirred together, stir in the champagne. **3** Let the ganache set up overnight according to the recipe directions.

Cupcakes **1** Prepare the Vanilla Bean Cupcake batter according to the recipe directions. **2** Reserve 12 large rose petals for decorating the finished cupcakes. Chop up the rest of the petals into little bits and fold them into the cupcake batter. **3** Bake the cupcakes according to the recipe directions. **4** Stir the rose flower water into the simple syrup. **5** When the cupcakes are hot from the oven, heavily soak them with the syrup.

Put It All Together **1** Frost each cupcake with a swirl of the champagne ganache. **2** Top each cupcake with one large, beautiful rose petal.

NOTE: Many natural food stores sell organic roses, and they'll sell you just the petals pretty cheap. Try to find the nicest-looking ones, because some will be used for decoration. The same store will probably also carry rose flower water.

SURLY TEMpLE

For some reason I had a fascination with mixed drinks when I was younger. I loved the Shirley Temple and always thought I was tough sh** strutting around with it until I realized there was no booze in it, so in went the vodka and the rest is history.

Cupcakes
1 recipe Vanilla Bean Cupcakes (page 16)

½ cup 7UP

1½ cups cherries, pitted and chopped
(see note)

1½ cups vodka

Frosting
1 recipe extra-thick Vanilla American
Buttercream (page 27)

2 cups powdered sugar

¼ cup grenadine

Put It All Together
12 beautiful, fresh cherries, stem on
if possible

HOW TO MAKE IT

Cupcakes **1** Prepare the Vanilla Bean Cupcake batter according to the recipe directions, but substitute the 7UP for the milk. **2** Once everything is mixed, fold in the cherries. **3** Bake the cupcakes according to the recipe directions. **4** When the cupcakes come out of the oven, while they're still hot, heavily soak them with the vodka.

Frosting **1** Prepare the Vanilla American Buttercream and make it extra thick by adding the extra powdered sugar. **2** Mix in the grenadine.

Put It All Together **1** Frost the cupcakes with the grenadine frosting. **2** Top each one with a cherry.

NOTE: If you really want to use maraschino cherries, it's okay, but organic ones aren't available. Good, fresh cherries from the farmer's market taste better.

WORLD TOuR

*****

OaxaCAN

The combination of spice and chocolate goes back to the Mayan traditions that actually began the idea of "drinking chocolate." If you've ever had Mexican hot chocolate, you know how intriguing and delicious spiced chocolate can be. The Oaxacan is an homage to this classic flavor combination, and we've found it to be an excellent way to introduce people to this flavor in a way that's not too "scary."

Cupcakes
3 tablespoons cayenne

1 tablespoon chipotle powder

¼ teaspoon black pepper

1 tablespoon cinnamon

1 recipe Devil's Food Cupcakes (page 19)

Frosting
1 recipe Ganache (page 30), at room temperature, *or* 1 recipe Chocolate American Buttercream (page 27) if you want to keep it vegan

HOW TO MAKE IT

Frosting **1** Prepare the ganache or the Chocolate American Buttercream according to the recipe directions.

Cupcakes **1** Prepare the Devil's Food Cupcake batter according to the recipe directions. To spice it up, add the cayenne, chipotle powder, black pepper, and cinnamon to the batter with the dry ingredients. **2** Bake the cupcakes according to the recipe directions.

Put It All Together **1** With a piping bag with a star tip, frost the cupcakes with room-temperature ganache or the chocolate buttercream. **2** Finish the cupcakes with a sprinkling of cayenne, both for color and to add a little spice to the ganache/buttercream.

White Chocolate Wasabi

A lot of my cupcakes seem to be somewhat controversial, but this one really made people ask a lot of questions. My answer is, "yes, it works." White chocolate and wasabi go incredibly well together. You just have to get over the initial "I don't get it."

Cupcakes
1 recipe Vanilla Bean Cupcakes
(page 16)

1 cup white chocolate pieces

Wasabi White Chocolate
2 cups chopped white chocolate

¼ cup wasabi powder (not wasabi paste—it will make the chocolate seize up)

Frosting
1 recipe Vanilla American Buttercream
(page 27)

1 cup Wasabi White Chocolate (see below)

HOW TO MAKE IT

Cupcakes **1** Prepare the Vanilla Bean Cupcake batter according to the recipe directions. **2** Stir in the white chocolate pieces. **3** Bake the cupcakes according to the recipe directions.

Wasabi White Chocolate **1** Over a double boiler, melt the white chocolate pieces. **2** Once the white chocolate is melted, mix in the wasabi powder. **3** Allow the chocolate to cool.

Frosting **1** Prepare the Vanilla American Buttercream according to the recipe directions. **2** Stir the cooled wasabi white chocolate into the buttercream with a rubber spatula.

Put It All Together **1** Dip the cupcakes into the remaining wasabi white chocolate and allow the chocolate to cool. **2** Frost the cupcakes with the wasabi buttercream. **3** Usually I top these with a white chocolate shaving, which you can make easily by shaving the side of a small block or bar of white chocolate with a vegetable peeler.

TANDOORI

Originally, this cupcake was made to mimic flavors we saw on a television cooking competition. Every week, we had a goal to use the top flavor components of that episode's winning dish and create a cupcake from them, no matter what. The Tandoori became the most popular one and was recently requested for a wedding cake!

Cupcakes

1 recipe Vanilla Bean Cupcakes (page 16)

1 mango, peeled and diced small

¼ cup diced fresh pineapple

4 tablespoons yellow curry

1 tablespoon grated fresh ginger

1 tablespoon cayenne

1 teaspoon asafoetida (available in Indian markets)

¼ teaspoon ground mustard

Frosting

1 recipe Vanilla American Buttercream (page 27)

2 tablespoons yellow curry

1 cup plain Greek yogurt (if you don't use Greek, strain the yogurt to thicken it)

¼ teaspoon cayenne

Cardamom Raisins

6 cardamom pods

1 cup golden raisins

2 cups water

HOW TO MAKE IT

Cardamom Raisins **1** In a saucepan, cover the cardamom pods and golden raisins with the water. Bring the water to a boil and then turn off the heat. **2** Set aside for at least one hour so the raisins can capture the essence of the cardamom. **3** Strain the raisins and toss out the cardamom pods.

Cupcakes **1** Prepare the Vanilla Bean Cupcake batter according to the recipe directions. **2** Fold the cardamom raisins into the batter along with the mango, pineapple, curry, ginger, cayenne, asafoetida, and ground mustard. **3** Bake the cupcakes according to the recipe directions.

Frosting **1** Prepare the Vanilla American Buttercream according to the recipe directions. **2** Fold the curry, yogurt, and cayenne to the buttercream with a rubber spatula.

Put It All Together **1** Frost the cooled cupcakes with the curried buttercream. **2** Usually I top these with some whole mustard seeds, but you can use a little cayenne or a candied ginger slice as well, or a cardamom pod for decoration.

HIBISCUS

My love for hibiscus flavor came from making hibiscus marshmallows at a candy business I owned a long time ago. I progressed from marshmallows to making hibiscus pancakes, and once we opened our bakery, the hibiscus cupcake came to life. Hibiscus has a floral cherry flavor, and once you get past the fact that it's a flower, it's really awesome and sort of playful.

Cupcakes
1 recipe Vanilla Bean Cupcakes (page 16)

hibiscus extract (see note)

2 to 3 drops pink food coloring (or a small amount of red food coloring)

Frosting
1 recipe Vanilla American Buttercream (page 27)

hibiscus extract (see note)

Put It All Together
1 recipe Lemon Curd (page 39)

12 strawberries

HOW TO MAKE IT

Cupcakes **1** Prepare the Vanilla Bean Cupcake batter according to the recipe directions, and add the hibiscus extract with the vanilla extract, according to the manufacturer's instructions. Add just enough food coloring to make the batter slightly pink. **2** Bake the cupcakes according to the recipe directions.

Frosting **1** Prepare the Vanilla American Buttercream according to the recipe directions and add the hibiscus extract to the Vanilla American Buttercream according to the manufacturer's instructions.

Put It All Together **1** Prepare the lemon curd according to the recipe directions. **2** Use your index finger to poke holes through the center of each cooled cupcake and fill the holes with the lemon curd. **3** Frost the cupcakes with the hibiscus buttercream and top each one with a strawberry.

NOTE: We use Amoretti brand of extract, but there are others available. Once you've got it, follow the manufacturer's instructions for how much to add, usually given in ratios, such as one tablespoon per cup of batter or buttercream, in this case.

CURRY CARDAMOM

Curry and chocolate really do go so well together. This cupcake was made originally as a wedding cake for a customer who worked at a spice shop, so the quality of the curry and the cardamom pods was key.

Cupcakes
1 recipe Vanilla Bean Cupcakes (page 16)
4 tablespoons high-quality curry powder
1 tablespoon garam masala
1 tablespoon minced fresh ginger

Ganache
1 recipe Ganache (page 30)
12 cardamom pods

HOW TO MAKE IT

Ganache **1** *Start the day before*—Begin preparing the ganache according to the recipe directions. Add the cardamom pods to the cream, then bring the cream to a boil. **2** Once the cream boils, remove it from the heat and allow the cardamom to steep for 1 hour. **3** Strain the pods out of the cream and bring the cream to a boil again. **4** Continue making the ganache according to the recipe directions.

Cupcakes **1** Prepare the Vanilla Bean Cupcake batter according to the recipe directions. **2** Mix the curry and garam masala into the batter, then fold in the fresh ginger. **3** Bake the cupcakes according to the recipe directions.

Put It All Together **1** Frost the cooled cupcakes with the cardamom ganache. **2** Top each cupcake with a toasted cardamom pod. If you can find golden cardamom pods, they're awesome toppers as well.

EARL GREY

Darker tea lends itself to dark chocolate really well. Usually I'd never combine dark chocolate with lemon, but this recipe just works and has come and gone as a favorite many times. It's a cupcake you can feel good about giving to Grandma.

Cupcakes
1 recipe Devil's Food Cupcakes (page 19)
½ cup Earl Grey tea leaves, chopped
2 tablespoons lemon zest

Ganache
1 recipe Ganache (page 30)
¼ cup Earl Grey tea leaves
½ cup honey (optional)

HOW TO MAKE IT

Ganache **1** *Start the day before*—Begin preparing the ganache according to the recipe directions. When the cream for the ganache boils, add the tea leaves and remove the pot from the heat. **2** Let the mixture steep for about 15 minutes and then strain the leaves out. It's important to not steep the tea leaves longer than 15 minutes because the cream will get bitter really fast. **3** Bring the cream back to a boil and pour it over the chocolate. **4** Finish the ganache according to the recipe directions. If you like honey in your tea, substitute honey for ½ cup cream, but do not heat up the honey; just add it to the bowl with the chocolate.

Cupcakes **1** Prepare the Devil's Food Cupcake batter according to the recipe directions and add the tea leaves and the lemon zest with the dry ingredients. Make sure the leaves are chopped really finely, or you'll end up with tea leaves stuck in your teeth. **2** Bake the cupcakes according to the recipe directions.

Put It All Together **1** Frost the cupcakes with the Earl Grey ganache. **2** You can top these cupcakes with candied lemon zest or a few tea leaves, for garnish.

GrEEN TEA WITH CANdIED RED BEANS

I am not the biggest fan of green tea as a drink; however, as a cupcake, WOW. I really love this recipe. We also made a cake that is similar and it became a bestseller fast.

Cupcakes
1 recipe Vanilla Bean Cupcakes (page 16)

4 tablespoons green tea powder (or finely chopped green tea leaves; see note)

2 tablespoons lemon zest

1 prepared recipe Candied Red Beans (see below), divided

Frosting
1 recipe Vanilla American Buttercream (page 27)

2 tablespoons ground ginger

1 tablespoon lemon zest

Candied Red Beans
1 (15-ounce) can red beans

1 recipe Simple Syrup (page 44)

HOW TO MAKE IT

Candied Red Beans **1** Drain the can of red beans into a sieve and wash the beans under cold running water. **2** Bring the simple syrup to a boil in a saucepan over high heat and add in the red beans. Let the beans simmer for a few minutes and then take them off the heat. **3** About an hour later, put the pan back on the heat and bring the mixture to a boil, then take it off the heat again. **4** Repeat Step 3, then drain and cool the beans.

Cupcakes **1** Prepare the Vanilla Bean Cupcake batter according to the recipe directions and add the green tea powder (or chopped green tea leaves) and the lemon with the dry ingredients. **2** Stir the candied red beans into the finished batter, reserving two dozen for garnish, if you'd like. **3** Bake the cupcakes according to the recipe directions.

Frosting **1** Prepare the Vanilla American Buttercream according to the recipe directions. **2** Add the ground ginger and the lemon zest.

Put It All Together **1** Frost the cupcakes with the ginger buttercream. **2** You can top each cupcake with candied red beans, candied ginger, or even candied lemon zest.

NOTE: Whether you use green tea powder or chopped green tea leaves really comes down to personal preference. I prefer the green tea powder.

CAPRESE

We briefly owned a bakery that specialized in odd and unique flavors. This cupcake was the most popular out of all we tried. Its legacy has lived on, and it has become a popular appetizer for weddings and various other parties. The most important thing to remember is to make these cupcakes when tomatoes and basil are at the peak of their season, otherwise they're really not as good.

Cupcakes
1 recipe Vanilla Bean Cupcakes (page 16)

2 cups chopped cherry or grape tomatoes

¼ cup minced basil

1 cup chopped fresh mozzarella in ¼-inch cubes

½ cup balsamic vinegar

1 recipe Simple Syrup (page 44)

Frosting
1 recipe extra-thick Vanilla American Buttercream (page 27)

2 cups powdered sugar

4 tablespoons minced basil

¼ cup balsamic vinegar

Put It All Together
12 cherry tomatoes, for garnish

HOW TO MAKE IT

Cupcakes **1** Prepare the Vanilla Bean Cupcake batter according to the recipe directions. **2** Fold in the tomatoes, basil, and mozzarella. **3** Bake the cupcakes according to the recipe directions. **4** Mix the balsamic vinegar into the simple syrup. **5** When the cupcakes are hot from the oven, lightly brush them with the syrup.

Frosting **1** Prepare the Vanilla American Buttercream according to the recipe directions and add the extra powdered sugar to make it extra thick. **2** Mix the basil and balsamic vinegar into the buttercream to bring it back to a regular frosting consistency.

Put It All Together **1** Using a piping bag with a big circle tip, place a dollop of buttercream onto each cupcake. **2** Finish each cupcake with a beautiful plump cherry tomato on top. If you feel like getting fancy, you can add a candied basil leaf to each cupcake for garnish.

Tres Leches with Roasted Pineapple

I absolutely love tres leches *cake; however, as I get older, I'm finding it difficult to eat because it's so heavy. (All that milk does not always do a body good.) This cupcake is my answer to that problem. The highlight is the roasted pineapple and the alternative milks, but I tried to stay true to tradition by using plain vanilla cake and frosting. You could try something else, but this is what seemed to work best. Make these about a day before you want to serve them—the milk needs about eight hours to properly soak into the cupcakes.*

Cupcakes
1 recipe Vanilla Bean Cupcakes (page 16)

Roasted Pineapple (see note)
1 pineapple

4 tablespoons butter

1 cup brown sugar

1 vanilla bean, scraped

Frosting
1 recipe Vanilla American Buttercream (page 27)

Tres Leches
1 cup whole milk

1 cup condensed milk

1 cup coconut milk

1 teaspoon cinnamon

HOW TO MAKE IT

Roasted Pineapple **1** Preheat the oven to 400°F. **2** Skin the pineapple, leaving it in one whole piece. **3** Heat up an oven-safe skillet and add the butter. Let the butter go past sizzling until it almost starts browning. **4** Place one side of the pineapple down on the pan and rotate it every 5 minutes until all sizes have browned a little. **5** Add the brown sugar and the scrapings from the vanilla bean to the pan. Let the sugar melt and the vanilla mingle in. **6** Transfer the whole skillet into the oven. Every few minutes, flip the pineapple and spoon the sugar syrup over the top. Take the pineapple out when it looks like caramel on the outside and is fluorescent yellow on the inside, about 20 minutes. **7** Let the pineapple cool and chop it into ½-inch cubes. Toss out the core in the middle—just cut around it.

Cupcakes **1** Prepare the Vanilla Bean Cupcakes according to the recipe directions.

Frosting **1** Prepare the Vanilla American Buttercream according to the recipe directions.

Tres Leches **1** In a medium bowl, combine the whole milk, condensed milk, and coconut milk, and add the cinnamon.

Put It All Together **1** Frost the cupcakes with the buttercream and place them in a dish with a lid. **2** Pour in the *tres leches* milk mixture, cover the cupcakes, and put them in the refrigerator. **3** The next day, spoon each cupcake into its own dish and sprinkle them with cubes of the roasted pineapple.

NOTE: This recipe will make too much roasted pineapple—way more than you need—but there's no reason to waste something so delicious. You can use it as a topping for ice cream or pizza, or just eat it by itself (that's what I do).

Fresh Herb and Lemon with Goat Cheese and Microgreens

This cupcake makes me really happy. It's sort of the culmination of the whole savory cupcake idea. I find that cupcakes like this work better as appetizers or intermezzos than as desserts, but I'd eat them no matter what. The secret to this one is that the goat cheese, the herbs, and the microgreens all need to be super fresh.

Cupcakes
1 cup goat cheese

1 recipe Vanilla Bean Cupcakes (page 16)

2 tablespoons minced fresh rosemary (see note)

1 tablespoon minced fresh thyme (see note)

1 tablespoon lemon zest

Frosting
1 recipe Vanilla American Buttercream (page 27)

2 cups goat cheese

Put It All Together
1 recipe Lemon Curd (page 39)

1 cup microgreens

HOW TO MAKE IT

Cupcakes **1** Preheat the oven to 400°F. **2** Crumble the goat cheese onto a baking sheet and bake it until it's browned and crunchy, about 10 minutes. Allow the goat cheese to cool. **3** Prepare the Vanilla Bean Cupcake batter according to the recipe directions. **4** Fold the baked goat cheese, rosemary, thyme, and lemon zest into the batter. **5** Bake the cupcakes according to the recipe directions.

Frosting **1** Prepare the Vanilla American Buttercream according to the recipe directions. **2** Soften the goat cheese in the microwave in 30-second intervals, just until it's spreadable. **3** Mix the goat cheese into the buttercream with a rubber spatula until the frosting is smooth.

Put It All Together **1** Prepare the lemon curd according to the recipe directions. **2** With your index finger, poke holes through the cupcakes and fill them with the lemon curd. **3** Frost the cupcakes with the goat cheese buttercream and top them with the microgreens.

NOTE: Instead of rosemary and thyme, you can substitute any seasonal fresh herbs you'd like.

LeMONGRASS

This cupcake sort of speaks for itself. It's very simple, but when you do it right and extract as much flavor from the lemongrass as you can, it's a real crowd pleaser.

Cupcakes
1 recipe Vanilla Bean Cupcakes (page 16)

1½ cups Lemongrass Simple Syrup (see below)

Frosting
1 recipe extra-thick Vanilla American Buttercream (page 27)

½ cup Lemongrass Simple Syrup (see below)

Lemongrass Simple Syrup
4 stalks lemongrass

6 cups water

4 cups sugar

HOW TO MAKE IT

Lemongrass Simple Syrup **1** Cut down 4 stalks of lemongrass (like you'd cut celery sticks). **2** Bring the lemongrass to a boil in a large pot of water. **3** Once the water is boiling, add the sugar, reduce the heat, and allow the mixture to simmer for about an hour.

Cupcakes **1** Prepare and bake the Vanilla Bean Cupcakes according to the recipe directions. **2** Heavily soak the cupcakes in the lemongrass simple syrup while they're still hot.

Frosting **1** Once the cupcakes are soaked with the lemongrass simple syrup, keep the remaining syrup simmering on the stove for another hour to reduce more liquid. You'll be left with something of a honey-like consistency. **2** Prepare the Vanilla American Buttercream according to the recipe directions. **3** Fold the thickened lemongrass syrup into the buttercream. Keep leftover syrup to add to mixed drinks.

Put It All Together **1** Frost the cupcakes with the lemongrass buttercream. **2** Top each one with a piece of candied lemongrass from the pot of syrup.

Thai Spice

I've seen so many people's eyes light up when they take a bite of this one. Someone ordered this flavor for their wedding but forgot to tell Grandma....I tried to catch her before she took a bite, but she ate the whole thing!

Cupcakes
4 tablespoons curry

2 tablespoons minced jalapeno

1 tablespoon minced fresh mint

1 tablespoon minced fresh cilantro

1 cup finely diced mango

1 recipe Vanilla Bean Cupcakes (page 16)

Put It All Together
2 cups Mango Curd (page 39)

fresh cilantro, for garnish

Frosting
1 cup Mango Curd (page 39)

1 recipe Vanilla American Buttercream (page 27)

HOW TO MAKE IT

Cupcakes **1** Prepare the Vanilla Bean Cupcake batter according to the recipe directions. **2** Mix the curry into the batter, then fold in the jalapeno, mint, cilantro, and mango. **3** Bake the cupcakes according to the recipe directions, and then allow them to cool.

Frosting **1** Prepare the mango curd according to the recipe directions. **2** Fold the mango curd into the Vanilla American Buttercream.

Put It All Together **1** With your index finger, poke holes in each cupcake and fill the holes with mango curd. **2** Frost the cupcakes with the mango buttercream. **3** Top each one with a sprig of fresh cilantro.

BLUE PLAtE SPECIAL

✦✦✦✦✦

WHITE TRASH

I'm adopted, and I know very little about my family except that they were from Joliet, Illinois, and a bit unsavory. I naturally sway toward trailer parks and NASCAR, love mullets and handlebar mustaches, and put mayo on everything. So this one goes out to my folks—I may not know you but, really, I feel like I do.

Cupcakes

½ recipe Marshmallow (page 42), chopped into ½-inch squares

1 cup (¼ recipe) All-Purpose Caramel (page 34)

1 recipe Devil's Food Cupcakes (page 19; it's the closest I get to boxed-mix flavor)

1 cup chopped salted pretzel sticks

1 cup chopped pecans

Frosting

1 recipe Vanilla American Buttercream (page 27)

Put It All Together

1 recipe Chocolate Sauce (page 38)

1 cup (¼ recipe) All-Purpose Caramel (page 34)

HOW TO MAKE IT

Cupcakes **1** Prepare the marshmallow according to the recipe directions. **2** Prepare the caramel according to the recipe directions. **3** Prepare the Devil's Food Cupcake batter according to the recipe directions. **4** Combine the pretzels, pecans, and marshmallow pieces in a bowl. Set aside half of the mixture. **5** Fold the caramel and the remaining pretzels, pecans, and marshmallows into the batter. **6** Bake the cupcakes according to the recipe directions.

Frosting **1** Prepare the Vanilla American Buttercream according to the recipe directions.

Put It All Together **1** Prepare the chocolate sauce according to the recipe directions. **2** Frost the cooled cupcakes with the buttercream. **3** Decorate the cupcake tops with a big heaps of the leftover pretzels, pecans, and marshmallows, then drizzle them with caramel and chocolate sauce.

BaCON PEANUT BUTTER

I was vegan for many years, and I was able to sway myself away from most meat, but bacon was one of those things that I continued to crave. I found it very hard to resist because it seems to lend itself well to so many applications and flavor combinations. The bacon-cupcake craze started a few years after the creation of this cupcake, so after years of people saying we were nuts, this cupcake has become our most popular.

Cupcakes
8 strips applewood-smoked bacon (we prefer Neuske's or Organic Valley brands)

1 recipe Devil's Food Cupcakes (page 19)

Frosting
2 cups chunky peanut butter

1 recipe Vanilla American Buttercream (page 27)

HOW TO MAKE IT

Cupcakes **1** Pan-fry the bacon strips or bake them in the oven. Either way, the cooked bacon must be crispy or it will cause the cupcakes to sour quickly. **2** Prepare the Devil's Food Cupcake batter according to the recipe directions. **3** Dice 6 bacon strips into little bits and mix them into the batter. **4** Bake the cupcakes according to the recipe directions. **5** Cut the remaining bacon strips into 1-inch pieces and degrease them with paper towels. Set aside.

Frosting **1** Prepare the Vanilla American Buttercream according to the recipe directions. **2** Fold in the peanut butter and mix well.

Put It All Together **1** Frost the cooled cupcakes with the peanut butter buttercream using a piping bag fitted with a large star tip (the peanuts may get caught in a smaller one). **2** Finish each cupcake with one thin slice of the reserved strips of bacon.

Chicago-Style Pizza

Yes, I'm from Chicago, and yes, we make the best pizza (and hot dogs). This cupcake combines all that I love about Chicago pizza, but makes it much easier to eat (and less messy).

Pizza Filling
½ recipe Vanilla Bean Cupcakes (page 16)
2 cups shredded provolone cheese

Frosting
2 cups marinara sauce (your favorite kind)
1 recipe Italian Buttercream (page 24)

Put It All Together
1 recipe Foncer Dough (page 43)
spray oil

1 pound (4 links) raw Italian sausage (your favorite kind)
1 cup marinara sauce

HOW TO MAKE IT

Pizza Filling **1** Prepare the Vanilla Bean Cupcake batter, but omit the vanilla extract and vanilla beans and use only ¹⁄₆ cup sugar. **2** Fold the cheese into the finished batter.

Frosting **1** Prepare the Italian Buttercream according to the recipe directions. While the sugar is whisking into the egg whites, slowly add the marinara sauce. Reserve a little of the sauce for putting it all together.

Put It All Together **1** Prepare the foncer dough according to the recipe directions. **2** Set a frying pan over high heat. Form the sausage into silver-dollar-sized patties. When the pan gets superhot, place the patties in the pan and press down on them while they're frying so they keep their shape. **3** Using a rolling pin, roll out the foncer dough just like pie dough on a floured surface. Stop when your dough gets to be about ¼-inch thick and cut out twelve 4-inch circles. **4** Spray the bottom of the cupcake pan with spray oil and fit the dough circles into each cup like a pie, and fold the edges over to create a thicker side wall. **5** Place a sausage patty at the bottom of each dough cup and then scoop the cupcake batter in. Top each one with a tablespoon of marinara.

6 Bake the cupcakes according to the Vanilla Bean Cupcake recipe directions. You are looking for the foncer dough to become a little golden and for the cupcakes to easily pop out of the pan. **7** Allow the cupcakes to cool on a wire rack and frost them with the marinara buttercream.

PaNCaKES aND BACON

Pancakes and bacon seem to satisfy me no matter what I'm actually craving, so a pancakes and bacon cupcake? Why not! The one important thing is to use thinly sliced bacon that is sweet rather than smoky. You want the sweetness and crispiness from the bacon more than a heavy smoke flavor.

Cupcakes
12 strips bacon, divided
1 recipe Vanilla Bean Cupcakes (page 16)
$^1/_3$ cup maple syrup

Frosting
1 recipe Italian Buttercream (page 24)
1 cup maple syrup

HOW TO MAKE IT

Cupcakes **1** Preheat the oven to 325°F. **2** Bake all 12 strips of bacon in the oven for about 30 minutes. **3** Prepare the Vanilla Bean Cupcake batter according to the recipe directions, but use only ¼ cup of milk. Instead of using all regular sugar, use only $^1/_3$ cup sugar and replace the rest with the maple syrup. **4** Chop up 8 strips of the bacon into small pieces and fold them into the cupcake batter. Reserve the remaining 4 strips for decorating the finished cupcakes. **5** Turn the oven up to 350°F, and bake the cupcakes according to the recipe directions.

Frosting **1** Prepare the Italian Buttercream according to the recipe directions, but substitute the maple syrup for the sugar and boil it according to the recipe directions, but for only about 2 minutes. **2** Continue making the buttercream as directed.

Put It All Together **1** Use a piping bag with a star tip to frost the cooled cupcakes with maple buttercream. **2** Top each cupcake with a long, skinny strip of bacon.

ROOT BEER FLOAT

I grew up in the Midwest, and on the weekends we went up to Wisconsin where we always visited one root beer stand that was awesome. So thank you, Wisconsin, for inspiring this recipe.

Cupcakes
1 recipe Chocolate Sponge Cupcakes
(page 22)

Ganache
1 recipe Ganache (page 30)

½ cup root beer

Frosting
1 recipe Vanilla American Buttercream
(page 27)

1 teaspoon root beer extract

Put It All Together
1 recipe Simple Syrup (page 44)

1 (12-ounce) bottle root beer
(I like Sprecher best)

12 Chocolate Cigarettes (page 37)

HOW TO MAKE IT

Ganache **1** *Start the day before*—Prepare the ganache according to the recipe directions, but omit ½ cup cream. **2** Heat the root beer with the remaining ½ cup cream, and proceed according to the recipe directions.

Cupcakes **1** Prepare the Chocolate Sponge Cupcakes according to the recipe directions.

Frosting **1** Prepare the Vanilla American Buttercream according to the recipe directions, and add the root beer extract with the vanilla extract.

Put It All Together **1** Prepare the simple syrup according to the recipe directions. **2** In a saucepan over high heat, bring the root beer to a boil and then reduce the heat. **3** Let the root beer simmer until it reduces by half, then add it to the simple syrup. **4** Prepare the chocolate cigarettes according to the recipe directions. **5** With your index finger, poke holes through the cupcakes and fill them with the root beer ganache. **6** Heavily soak each cupcake with the root beer simple syrup. **7** Using an ice cream scoop, scoop the buttercream on top of each one and stick a chocolate cigarette right into the center like a straw.

AVOCADO AND BLACK PEPPER

For as long as I can remember, I've loved the combination of avocado, pepper, and balsamic vinegar. I must've eaten at some fancy place as a child because it really stuck with me. My stint in Amsterdam opened my mind to savory baking and gave me the confidence to make this cupcake.

Cupcakes
2 tablespoons whole black peppercorns
1 recipe Vanilla Bean Cupcakes (page 16)
1 recipe Simple Syrup (page 44)
½ cup balsamic vinegar

Frosting
2 medium-sized super-ripe (but not browning) avocados
2 tablespoons lime juice
1 recipe Vanilla American Buttercream (page 27)

HOW TO MAKE IT

Cupcakes **1** Grind the peppercorns in a pepper grinder. **2** Prepare the Vanilla Bean Cupcake batter according to the recipe directions and add the ground pepper with the dry ingredients. **3** Bake the cupcakes according to the recipe directions. **4** Prepare the simple syrup according to the recipe directions, then mix in the balsamic vinegar. **5** When the cupcakes are hot from the oven, soak them with the syrup.

Frosting **1** The ripeness of your avocado is vital to this frosting. Choose two perfect avocados, purée them in a food processor, then add the lime juice. The lime will add a little tang and help the avocado keep its color. Purée the mixture until it's smooth. **2** Prepare the Vanilla American Buttercream according to the recipe directions, then mix in the avocado purée.

Put It All Together **1** Frost each cupcake with a star-tip swirl of avocado buttercream. **2** If you have any spare peppercorns, you can sprinkle one or two on top of each cupcake.

"THE" RED VELVET

By far, this cupcake has been our bestseller. It's simple and to the point, and it drives people crazy.

Cupcakes

3 cups all-purpose flour

1½ cups sugar

¼ teaspoon baking soda

¼ teaspoon salt

¼ cup cocoa powder

1½ cups vegetable oil (I like sunflower oil the best)

¾ cup buttermilk

½ cup superhot water (this helps keep the cupcakes moist)

red food coloring (or beet powder—it's better for you) to taste (see note)

Frosting

1 recipe Cream Cheese Frosting (page 28)

HOW TO MAKE IT

Cupcakes **1** Preheat the oven to 350°F and line a cupcake pan with cupcake liners. **2** Mix together the flour, sugar, baking soda, salt, and cocoa powder in a large mixing bowl. **3** In a medium mixing bowl, whisk together the oil, buttermilk, and hot water, and pour the mixture into the large mixing bowl with the dry ingredients. **4** Whisk all the ingredients together until they're combined and there are no lumps. **5** Add the red food coloring a little bit at a time until the batter is your desired redness. Mix with the rubber spatula so you don't overmix it. **6** With the ice cream scoop, fill the cups in the cupcake pan about ¾ full and bake for

15 minutes or until a toothpick comes out clean (or the middle of the cupcake bounces back when you press it gently).

Frosting **1** Prepare the cream cheese frosting according to the recipe directions.

Put It All Together **1** Slice the tops off the cooled cupcakes at the rim of the cupcake cup with a serrated knife. **2** Using a piping bag with a big round tip, squeeze out a large dollop of frosting into the center of the cupcake. **3** Place the tops of the cupcakes on top of the frosting to make cupcake sandwiches. Doing this adds a cool look but, more importantly, it keeps the cupcakes moist. You can put powdered sugar on top for decoration or just leave the cupcakes plain. I've found that most people like their red velvet straight and to the point, but we put a little powdered-sugar checkerboard pattern on ours.

NOTE: These cupcakes get a harder crust than some, which some people like. If you don't, you can do one of two things: (1) cut it off, or (2) wrap the cupcakes overnight in plastic wrap so the tops will soften.

NOTE: The color of red food coloring varies from brand to brand, so the amount you add will depend on how red you want your cupcakes to be. Organic colors don't bake as well as conventional ones (they turn brown), so the beet powder is a good alternative, although it will alter the flavor of the cupcakes a little and they won't get as bright red as they would with conventional colors.

CORN DOG

I think my corn dog fascination comes from my love of carnies…but it could also be because I love food on sticks. Either way, this one's great!

Cupcakes

1 recipe Vanilla Bean Cupcakes (page 16)

2 cups coarse cornmeal or polenta

4 all-beef hotdogs (Vienna beef if you're from around Chicago), cooked

Frosting

1 recipe Italian Buttercream (page 24)

1 cup ketchup

HOW TO MAKE IT

Cupcakes **1** Prepare the Vanilla Bean Cupcake batter according to the recipe directions, but omit the vanilla extract and vanilla beans. Add the cornmeal with the dry ingredients. **2** Cut the hot dogs into coin-sized slices, and fold the pieces into the finished batter. **3** Bake the cupcakes according to the recipe directions, and allow them to cool.

Frosting **1** Prepare the Italian Buttercream according to the recipe directions, and when it's almost completely whisked together, slowly add the ketchup to the mixer.

Put It All Together **1** Frost the cupcakes with the ketchup buttercream. **2** Decorate each cupcake with a skewer stuck through the top.

PiNK LEMOnaDE

We have one wholesale customer who really keeps us on our toes with cupcake flavors. This one was a specific request from them, and it proved to be very popular.

Cupcakes
1 recipe Vanilla Bean Cupcakes (page 16)
½ cup fresh raspberries

Frosting
1 recipe Vanilla American Buttercream (page 27)
¼ cup lemon juice
1 tablespoon lemon zest

Put It All Together
1 recipe Lemon Curd (page 39)

HOW TO MAKE IT

Cupcakes **1** Purée the raspberries in a food processor until it has the consistency of a really loose jam. **2** Prepare the Vanilla Bean Cupcake batter according to the recipe directions, but leave out the milk and replace it with ¼ cup raspberry purée. **3** Bake the cupcakes according to the recipe directions.

Frosting **1** Prepare the Vanilla American Buttercream according to the recipe directions, but replace the milk with the lemon juice. **2** Add the lemon zest to the finished buttercream.

Put It All Together **1** Prepare the lemon curd according to the recipe directions. **2** With your index finger, poke holes through the cupcakes and fill the holes with the lemon curd. **3** Frost the cupcakes with the lemonade buttercream. **4** Top each cupcake with a fresh raspberry.

BBQ PORK CUPCAKE

I was recently visited by a girl who had the idea for a cupcake similar to this one. We spoke about it for a while, but what she didn't know is that we were already making this in the next room on the same day! Instead of apple pie on the fourth of July, we offered BBQ cupcakes. I store these in the fridge and microwave them for a few seconds when people order them so the butter melts a little and the cake softens. It really is awesome!

Cupcakes
1 recipe Vanilla Bean Cupcakes (page 16)

2 cups shredded BBQ pork (see note)

2 cups fresh corn

Maple Butter
¼ cup maple syrup

2 cups butter, softened

Put It All Together
2 cups shredded BBQ pork (see note)

HOW TO MAKE IT

Cupcakes **1** Prepare the Vanilla Bean Cupcake batter according to the recipe directions. **2** Fold the pork into the batter, then fold in the corn. **3** Bake the cupcakes according to the recipe directions.

Maple Butter **1** In lieu of frosting on these cupcakes, we put a swirl of whipped maple butter on top. Whip your favorite maple syrup into the butter with a standing mixer with a paddle attachment.

Put It All Together **1** Top each cupcake with a swirl of whipped maple butter. **2** Press a tablespoon or so of the pork into the top of each cupcake.

NOTE: There are two ways you can go about getting pork: You can make your own BBQ sauce and pork, or you can buy them. There are plenty of natural foods stores around us that sell amazing BBQ pork, and since I'm not a deli, I buy mine. You just need to choose the best quality around and you'll be fine.

THANKSGIVING

I made this cupcake sort of as a joke. As a baker, I never get real holidays. I always have to spend them at the bakery and take time off (maybe) in January. I made this cupcake for myself so I could remember what Thanksgiving tasted like. However, we sold a few and they quickly developed a following. Soon it was nominated to be best cupcake in Chicago of 2008! Who would have known?

Cupcakes
1 pound sweet potatoes

2 tablespoons raw sugar

4 tablespoons flour

2 tablespoons butter or soy margarine
(to keep it vegan)

1 recipe Vanilla Bean Cupcakes (page 16)

Cranberry Relish
3 cups fresh cranberries

½ cup sugar

2 tablespoons orange zest

Frosting
1 recipe French Meringue (page 32)

HOW TO MAKE IT

Cupcakes **1** Peel and boil the sweet potatoes until they're soft. Allow them to cool and then chop or purée them in a food processor (but you don't want this to be puréed like baby food—there should be chunks left, like sweet potatoes at Thanksgiving dinner). **2** Preheat the oven to 350°F. **3** In a bowl, mix the sugar, flour and butter together with your fingers until the mixture is mealy in texture, but with some pea-sized pieces left. **4** Bake the sugar mixture on a baking sheet for about 15 minutes to make streusel. Let the streusel cool and then break it up with your fingers. **5** Prepare the Vanilla Bean Cupcake batter according to the recipe directions, then fold in the sweet potato purée. **6** Once the cupcake batter is in the cupcake tray, top each cup with the streusel so they have a nice, sweet crunch on top when they bake. **7** Bake the cupcakes according to the recipe directions.

Cranberry Relish **1** Place the cranberries, sugar, and orange zest into a stock pot over low heat. **2** Cook the mixture until the sugar is dissolved and the cranberries have popped and started to thicken, about 15 to 20 minutes.

Frosting **1** Prepare the French meringue according to the recipe directions.

Put It All Together **1** With your index finger, poke holes in the tops of the cupcakes and fill them with the cranberry relish. **2** Top each cupcake with a big dollop of French meringue and toast it with a crème brûlée torch.

MOUNTAIN DEW

A while back I was asked to make a giant replica of a Mountain Dew can out of cake. I thought it would be pretty cool if the cake matched the flavor, so I came up with these cupcakes for the taste test. They won over the customers, who booked the cake!

Cupcakes
1 recipe Vanilla Bean Cupcakes (page 16)
2 cups Mountain Dew, divided

Frosting
1 recipe Vanilla American Buttercream (page 27)
2 cups powdered sugar
1¼ cups Mountain Dew

Put It All Together
green food coloring
yellow food coloring

HOW TO MAKE IT

Cupcakes **1** Prepare the Vanilla Bean Cupcake batter according to the recipe directions, but replace ¼ cup of the milk with ¼ cup Mountain Dew. **2** Bake the cupcakes according to the recipe directions. **3** When the cupcakes come out of the oven, heavily douse them with the remaining Mountain Dew.

Frosting **1** Prepare the Vanilla American Buttercream according to the recipe directions, but add the 2 cups powdered sugar to make it extra thick. **2** In the standing mixer with the paddle attachment, slowly add the Mountain Dew to the extra-thick buttercream until the correct consistency of regular (not extra-thick) buttercream is achieved. Pour the Mountain Dew in slowly, or the buttercream will trick you and become too loose.

Put It All Together **1** Dye half the buttercream green and the other half yellow, and put them side by side in a piping bag. **2** Swirl the frosting onto the tops of the cupcakes.

PEANUT BUTTER AND JELLY

This cupcake is pretty self-explanatory and very delicious. I've found that adults like it more than children (who usually just go for sprinkles).

Cupcakes
1 recipe Vanilla Bean Cupcakes (page 16)

Frosting
1 recipe Vanilla American Buttercream (page 27)

2 cups chunky peanut butter

Put It All Together
2 cups fruit jam (make or buy your favorite—I usually use strawberry)

HOW TO MAKE IT

Cupcakes **1** Prepare the Vanilla Bean Cupcakes according to the recipe directions.

Frosting **1** Prepare the Vanilla American Buttercream according to the recipe directions. **2** Fold the peanut butter into the buttercream.

Put It All Together **1** With your index finger, poke holes through the cupcakes and fill them with the jam. **2** Frost the cupcakes with peanut butter buttercream and a dollop of jam.

THE ELVIS

After I wrote this recipe, I found out that a TON of people have written Elvis cupcake recipes. I pondered changing the name, but I'm pretty sure the King would have liked mine the best, so I kept it.

Cupcakes
6 strips bacon
1 recipe Devil's Food Cupcakes (page 19)
2 bananas

Put It All Together
12 banana chips

Frosting
1 recipe Vanilla American Buttercream (page 27)
2 cups chunky peanut butter

HOW TO MAKE IT

Cupcakes **1** Preheat the oven to 350°F. **2** Bake the bacon on a baking sheet until the strips are crunchy but not burned, about 25 minutes. Then drain all the grease off and allow the bacon to cool. **3** When the bacon is cool, mince the strips up into little pieces. Reserve half the minced bacon for garnish. **4** Prepare the Devil's Food Cupcake batter according to the recipe directions. **5** Slice the bananas into thin rounds. Fold the banana slices and the remaining bacon into the cupcake batter. **6** Bake the cupcakes according to the recipe directions.

Frosting **1** Prepare the Vanilla American Buttercream according to the recipe directions. **2** Add the peanut butter to the buttercream with a rubber spatula and mix well.

Put It All Together **1** Using a piping bag with a star tip, frost the cupcakes with peanut butter buttercream. **2** Sprinkle the cupcakes with the reserved bacon pieces. **3** Top each cupcake with a banana chip and you're done!

PUNKIN' DONUTS

Growing up, I was one of those punk rock street kids that some neighborhoods in Chicago are infamous for, and we particularly liked to hang out at a certain donut shop. This cupcake is dedicated to all the free donuts they graciously gave me, and to Officer Sweeney, who just loved to give me sh**.

Cupcakes
1 recipe Vanilla Bean Cupcakes (page 16)

Raspberry Filling
4 cups fresh raspberries

1 cup sugar

Frosting
1 recipe Chocolate American Buttercream (page 27)

Donut Glaze
4 cups powdered sugar, sifted

½ cup heavy cream (or soymilk if you want it vegan)

HOW TO MAKE IT

Raspberry Filling **1** Combine the raspberries and sugar in a saucepan. **2** Cook the mixture over high heat, stirring until a jam consistency forms. **3** Remove the pot from the heat and set the filling aside to cool.

Cupcakes **1** Prepare the Vanilla Bean Cupcakes according to the recipe directions.

Frosting **1** Prepare the Chocolate American Buttercream according to the recipe directions.

Donut Glaze **1** In a mixing bowl, whisk the powdered sugar and cream together until the powdered sugar is totally dissolved. For a thicker glaze, add a little more powdered sugar; for a thinner glaze, add more cream.

Put It All Together **1** Use your index finger to poke holes through the centers of the cupcakes, and fill the holes with jam, using a teaspoon. **2** With a piping bag with a large round tip, make a swirl of buttercream on top of each cupcake. **3** Freeze the cupcakes for about 15 minutes, then remove them from the freezer and dip them into the donut glaze. **4** Garnish with sprinkles if you'd like.

fARM TO tABLE

★★★★★

BLACKBERRY LEMON

This cupcake is a summer favorite. I've paired it with a cream cheese frosting, but it also goes well with Italian or American buttercream with a little lemon oil mixed in.

Cupcakes
1 recipe Lemon Cupcake batter (page 23)
3 cups roughly chopped blackberries

Frosting
1 recipe Cream-Cheese Frosting (page 28)
4 tablespoons lemon zest

Put It All Together
12 blackberries, for garnish

HOW TO MAKE IT

Cupcakes **1** Prepare the Lemon Cupcake batter according to the recipe directions. **2** Fold the blackberries into the batter. **3** Bake the cupcakes according to the recipe directions.

Frosting **1** Prepare the cream cheese frosting according to the recipe directions. **2** Mix the lemon zest into the frosting with a rubber spatula.

Put It All Together **1** Frost the cupcakes with a big dollops of the frosting. **2** Top each cupcake with a whole blackberry. If you're serving these right away, you can put some fresh lemon zest or even candied lemon peel on top as well.

NOTE: Depending on the season, if raspberries look better than blackberries, you can use them in this recipe instead.

STRAWBERRY SHORTCAKE

Truth be told, I just love this one, but I'm really one of those fruity-dessert types of people. The fresh strawberries really make this cupcake shine. Wait to make these until you can find ripe strawberries at your local farmer's market—it makes all the difference.

Cupcakes
1 recipe Vanilla Bean Cupcakes (page 16)
3 cups halved fresh strawberries

Frosting
1 recipe Vanilla American Buttercream (page 27)
1 vanilla bean, scraped

HOW TO MAKE IT

Cupcakes **1** Prepare the Vanilla Bean Cupcake batter according to the recipe directions. **2** Fold the strawberries into the batter. **3** Bake the cupcakes according to the recipe directions.

Frosting **1** Prepare the Vanilla American Buttercream according to the recipe directions, but while it's mixing, toss in the scrapings from the vanilla bean.

Put It All Together **1** Using a piping bag with a star tip, frost the cupcakes with the buttercream. **2** Top each cupcake with a halved strawberry. If you're making these ahead of time, put the strawberry with the cut side down; if you're making them "to order," they look beautiful with the strawberry face up.

COCONUT MANGO

I'm not fond of coconut, but I cannot deny my customers what they ask for. Tropical flavors are huge, and I think they give people a little sense of "vacation" during their regular routine. This cupcake was spawned from a wedding cake recipe and instantly became a hit. The addition of the mango curd helps to keep the cupcake moist even when it needs to sit overnight or for a day.

Cupcakes
1 cup butter, softened

2 cups sugar

3 cups flour

2 teaspoons salt

2 teaspoons baking powder

1 cup coconut milk

1 cup coconut cream

6 egg whites (no little yolk bits), at room temperature

Put It All Together
1 cup (½ recipe) Mango Curd (page 39)

fresh coconut, toasted and sliced, for garnish

Frosting
1 cup (½ recipe) Mango Curd (page 39)

1 recipe Cream Cheese Frosting (page 28), slightly chilled

HOW TO MAKE IT

Cupcakes **1** Preheat the oven to 350°F and line a cupcake pan with cupcake liners. **2** In a standing mixer with the paddle attachment, mix the butter and sugar together until light and fluffy, about 10 to 15 minutes, then scrape down the sides of the bowl. **3** In a medium bowl, mix the flour, salt, and baking powder together.

In a separate medium bowl, mix the coconut milk and coconut cream together. **4** Slowly alternate adding the dry ingredients with the coconut liquids to the standing mixer. Stop a few times to scrape down the sides of the bowl. Once all the ingredients have been placed in the bowl, turn the mixer on high for just a few seconds to wake up the batter a little, but not so much as to overmix it. **5** Set the batter aside in a large mixing bowl and wash the bowl from the standing mixer well (fat breaks down egg whites—they really hate each other—so if any butter fat is left in the bowl, the next step won't work). **6** In the standing mixer with the whip attachment, whisk the egg whites until soft peaks form, about 5 minutes. Egg whites really like to whip when they're at least at room temperature, if not warmer; the colder they are they longer they'll take to whip. If you're in a hurry, you can always warm them in a bowl over simmering water while keeping them moving with a spatula. If you choose this method, you have to stand there and actually pay attention to them or you'll end up with a bowl of cooked egg whites. Soft peaks should form quickly under the right conditions. If you're scared, whipping them too little is fine, but overwhipped egg whites won't work well. So when in doubt, slightly underwhip. You'll get better at it, I promise. **7** Once you have the egg whites whipped and the batter made, slowly fold the whites into the batter, a little bit at a time, with a rubber spatula. Don't go crazy with this. If you deflate the egg whites, they won't help give the cupcakes structure and they'll sink in the middle. **8** Scoop the batter into the cupcake pan with the ice cream scoop, filling the cups in the cupcake pan about ¾ full and bake for about 15 minutes or until a toothpick comes out clean.

Frosting **1** Prepare the mango curd according to the recipe directions and allow it to cool. **2** Prepare the cream cheese frosting according to the recipe directions. **3** Fold the cooled curd into the frosting.

Put It All Together **1** Poke holes through the cupcakes using your index finger and fill the holes with spoonfuls of the mango curd. **2** Frost the cupcakes with the mango frosting. **3** Top each cupcake with toasted slices of fresh coconut.

STRAWBERRY RHUBARB

Come on now, what could be more vintage and classic in baking than strawberry rhubarb? Personally I like rhubarb more than strawberries, so I go heavy on the rhubarb, but you can use less if you'd like.

Cupcakes
2 cups diced rhubarb, in ¼-inch cubes
½ cup sugar
1 recipe Vanilla Bean Cupcakes (page 16)
2 cups strawberries, quartered

Put It All Together
12 little strawberries

Frosting
1 recipe Vanilla American Buttercream (page 27)
2 cups powdered sugar
1 cup strawberry jam

HOW TO MAKE IT

Cupcakes **1** In a sauté pan over medium heat, sauté the rhubarb in the sugar until the rhubarb is still crunchy and bright red on the outside but softer on the inside, about 5 minutes. You're just cooking it a little—you don't want the rhubarb to get mushy or turn brown. **2** Take the rhubarb off the heat and strain it in a colander. Make sure you strain all the liquid out or the cupcakes won't rise. **3** Put the rhubarb on a cookie sheet to cool. **4** Prepare the Vanilla Bean Cupcake batter according to the recipe directions. **5** Fold the strawberry quarters and the cooled rhubarb into the batter. **6** Bake the cupcakes according to the recipe directions.

Frosting **1** Prepare the Vanilla American Buttercream according to the recipe directions, but add the additional 2 cups powdered sugar to make it extra thick. **2** Fold the strawberry jam into the buttercream.

Put It All Together **1** Frost the cooled cupcakes with the strawberry buttercream. **2** Top each cupcake with a strawberry.

ROASTED BANANA WITH RICOTTA

This cupcake was made on a dare, and it has become one of our most popular cupcakes to date. The roasted bananas add a lot of moisture, and the ricotta puts a twist on the traditional buttercream frosting.

Cupcakes
1 recipe Vanilla Bean Cupcakes (page 16)

2 bananas

2 tablespoons butter

¼ cup brown sugar

Frosting
1 recipe Vanilla American Buttercream (page 27)

2 cups fresh ricotta

1 tablespoon lemon zest (optional)

Put It All Together
banana chips, for garnish

HOW TO MAKE IT

Cupcakes **1** Prepare the Vanilla Bean Cupcake batter according to the recipe directions and set it aside.
2 To roast the bananas, melt the butter in a sauté pan on high heat. Slice the bananas into thin disks and lay the disks in one layer in the butter. Keep the bananas moving so they don't stick and after about 1 minute, flip them over and let them cook for an additional minute. Both sides should be slightly brown. Cover the bananas with brown sugar and sauté until the sugar is melted. **3** Allow the roasted bananas to cool and then fold them into the cupcake batter with a rubber spatula. **4** Bake the cupcakes according to the recipe directions.

Frosting **1** Prepare the Vanilla American Buttercream according to the recipe directions. **2** Fold the ricotta and lemon zest, if using, into the buttercream with a rubber spatula.

Put It All Together **1** Pipe the buttercream onto the cooled cupcakes with a piping bag with a star tip.
2 Top each cupcake with a banana chip.

OrANGE BLoSSOM

This recipe is a bit more adult than a more traditional orange cream cupcake. The flower water is a little perfumey, but when used in the right amounts, it actually adds a lot of depth and makes the cupcake stand out.

Cupcakes
1 recipe Vanilla Bean Cupcakes (page 16)
½ cup finely chopped orange zest
1 recipe Simple Syrup (page 44)
4 tablespoons orange flower water

Frosting
1 recipe Vanilla American Buttercream (page 27)
2 tablespoons orange zest
1 tablespoon orange oil

HOW TO MAKE IT

Cupcakes **1** Prepare the Vanilla Bean Cupcake batter according to the recipe directions. **2** Add the orange zest to the cupcake batter. **3** Bake the cupcakes according to the recipe directions. **4** Mix together the simple syrup and the orange flower water. **5** When the cupcakes come out of the oven, brush the tops with syrup while they're still hot so the syrup soaks in, then set the cupcakes aside to cool.

Frosting **1** Prepare the Vanilla American Buttercream according to the recipe directions. **2** Fold the orange zest and orange oil into the buttercream.

Put It All Together **1** Frost the cooled cupcakes with the orange-scented frosting using a pastry bag with a star tip. **2** Usually I top these cupcakes with edible flowers or candied violets, but you can also top them with candied orange peel or fresh orange zest if you'll be eating them right away.

NOTE: If you really want to get all fancy, you could make a batch of orange curd (see Lemon Curd, page 39) and fill the cupcakes with that. Doing this would also add moisture and lengthen the shelf life of the cupcakes.

THE INFAMOUS SPINACH AND APPLE

Truth be told, it was my mentor in Amsterdam who inspired this cupcake with his spinach and apple roulade. His cake was a huge hit in Europe, as I believe this cupcake would be. When we opened Chaos Theory, our former evil-twin bakery, this cupcake took everyone by surprise, but we still get orders for it, so maybe it does have a place here.

Cupcakes
6 cups spinach
1 recipe Vanilla Bean Cupcakes (page 16)

Frosting
2 tablespoons butter
2 cups minced purple onions (see note)
1 recipe Vanilla American Buttercream (page 27)

Sautéed Apples
3 cups chopped apples
2 tablespoons butter
2 tablespoons sugar

HOW TO MAKE IT

Cupcakes **1** Steam the spinach in a large pot just until the spinach is wilted and turns bright green.
2 Strain the spinach in a colander and squeeze out any remaining water. Purée the spinach in a food processor and then strain it again. **3** Prepare the Vanilla Bean Cupcake batter according to the recipe directions.
4 Fold the puréed spinach into the batter. **5** Bake the cupcakes according to the recipe directions.
Frosting **1** Melt the butter in a sauté pan, then add the minced onions. Cook the onions until they're a little past the translucent stage but are only slightly caramelized. **2** Line a cookie sheet with paper towels and lay the onions on top so the towels absorb the excess fat and the onions cool more quickly. **3** Prepare the Vanilla American Buttercream according to the recipe directions. **4** Purée the cooled onions in a food processor, then mix them into the buttercream.

Sautéed Apples **1** Dice the apples into small, even pieces, about ¼-inch cubes. **2** Over medium heat, melt the butter in a sauté pan. When the butter starts to brown, toss in the apples. Move them around a bit in the pan and toss in the sugar—not a lot, just enough to give the apples a little boost. **3** Pour the apples out onto a baking sheet to cool.

Put It All Together **1** Using the piping bag with the star tip, pipe a big circle of frosting around the cupcake tops. **2** Fill the circles of frosting with the sautéed apples.

NOTE: You can use regular red onions for this, but if you happen to be by a farmer's market during onion season, buy yourself some of the long purple-stalk onions. They're sweeter and add a lot more flavor to the finished cupcake.

CANDIED WHITE BEAN WITH GRAPEFRUIT

On a trip to New York, I went to one restaurant that paired grapefruit and white beans together for a dessert that ended up being one of the best things I've ever tasted. I was incredibly inspired and knew I had to use the flavors. Out came this cupcake.

Cupcakes
1 recipe Simple Syrup (page 44)

1 (12-ounce) can white beans

1 recipe Vanilla Bean Cupcake batter (page 16)

Put It All Together
1 recipe Grapefruit Curd (page 39)

Frosting
1 recipe Vanilla American Buttercream (page 27)

2 tablespoons grapefruit juice

HOW TO MAKE IT

Cupcakes **1** Bring the simple syrup to a boil in a saucepan. Strain and rinse the white beans and add them to the boiling syrup. **2** Allow the beans to boil in the syrup for about a minute, then turn the flame off. Let the mixture cool and then bring it to a boil again. The cooked beans should be translucent. **3** Prepare the Vanilla Bean Cupcake batter according to the recipe directions. **4** Thoroughly strain the beans. Reserve 24 candied beans for garnish and fold the rest into the cupcake batter. **5** Bake the cupcakes according to the recipe directions.

Frosting **1** Prepare the Vanilla American Buttercream according to the recipe directions, but omit the vanilla and replace it with the grapefruit juice.

Put It All Together **1** Prepare the grapefruit curd according to the recipe directions. **2** With your index finger, poke holes through the tops of all the cupcakes and fill the holes with the grapefruit curd. **3** Frost the cupcakes with grapefruit frosting and top each one with a few of the reserved candied white beans.

SeRiOUSLY KiLLER BaNaNa

Some flavors are just classic, and banana is one of them. For as long as baking as an art (and sport) has existed, so has the use of bananas for both flavor and moisture. We use this recipe for cakes and cupcakes, as well as for banana bread. It's dense but moist, with just the right amount of sweetness. For a twist, try adding chocolate chips or candied pecans to the batter.

Cupcakes

¼ cup whole milk

¼ teaspoon lemon juice

1 cup shortening (I prefer palm fruit)

2 cups sugar

4 eggs, beaten

1 tablespoon vanilla extract

4½ cups all-purpose flour

2 teaspoons baking soda

2 tablespoons baking powder

2 teaspoons salt

2 cups mashed ripened banana (it's easiest to just mash it with a fork)

Frosting

1 recipe Chocolate American Buttercream (page 27)

HOW TO MAKE IT

Cupcakes **1** Preheat the oven to 350°F and line a cupcake pan with cupcake liners. **2** In a small bowl, mix the milk with the lemon juice and set aside. This makes a poor man's buttermilk. **3** In a standing mixer using the paddle attachment, cream the shortening and sugar together until light and fluffy, about 10 to 15 minutes. **4** Scrape down the sides of the bowl and add the eggs and vanilla, and mix slowly to combine. The mixture will look broken, but don't get scared. **5** In the medium bowl, mix together the flour, baking soda, baking powder, and salt. **6** Add the mashed banana to the mixer, then slowly alternate adding the dry ingredients and the milk mixture. Once all the ingredients are incorporated and the bowl sides have been scraped down, give the batter one quick last pulse at the highest speed for just a few seconds. **7** Using the ice cream scoop, fill the cups in the cupcake pan about ¾ full and bake for about 15 minutes or until a toothpick comes out clean (not until it comes out dry—this is a very moist batter, and you don't want to see streaks of batter on the toothpick).

Frosting **1** Prepare the Chocolate American Buttercream according to the recipe directions.

Put It All Together **1** Using a piping bag with a star tip, frost the cooled cupcakes with the buttercream.

Apple Spice

This is apple pie in cupcake form, made even better with brown sugar frosting. I've thought about adding cheddar cheese for all you Wisconsinites, but I'll leave that up to you.

Cupcakes
3 cups chopped apples

2 tablespoons butter

2 tablespoons sugar

1 recipe Vanilla Bean Cupcakes (page 16)

1 tablespoon cinnamon

1 teaspoon ground cloves

1 teaspoon ground allspice

½ teaspoon ground nutmeg

Frosting
1 recipe Vanilla American Buttercream (page 27)

1 cup brown sugar

HOW TO MAKE IT

Cupcakes **1** Dice the apples into small, even pieces, about ¼-inch cubes. **2** Over medium heat, melt the butter in a sauté pan. When the butter starts to brown, toss in the apples. Move them around a bit in the pan and toss in the sugar to give the apples a boost. **3** Pour the apples out onto a baking sheet to cool. **4** Prepare the Vanilla Bean Cupcake batter according to the recipe directions, but add the cinnamon, cloves, allspice, and nutmeg with the dry ingredients. **5** Fold the apples into the batter. Reserve the apple juice and about a cup of apples for garnish. **6** Bake the cupcakes according to the recipe directions.

Frosting **1** Prepare the Vanilla American Buttercream according to the recipe directions. **2** Stir the brown sugar into the buttercream with a rubber spatula.

Put It All Together **1** Brush the warm cupcakes with the reserved apple juice. **2** Using a piping bag with a star tip, make a big frosting circle around the top of the cupcakes. **3** Fill the circles with the reserved apples.

CREAMSICLE

We made this cupcake for a wedding and came home with rave reviews. I know, I know what you're thinking—"But it's just a creamsicle, everyone makes those!" Yes, they do, but ours is different. Everyone else uses a chemical-based orange extract. We do not. Orange flavor exists in real life, so why use a chemical ripoff? So here's our "made with real oranges" creamsicle cupcake.

Cupcakes
1 recipe Vanilla Bean Cupcakes (page 16)

1⅛ cups fresh orange juice, divided

zest of 6 oranges

1 recipe Simple Syrup (page 44)

1 cup fresh orange juice

Frosting
1 recipe Vanilla American Buttercream (page 27)

2 vanilla beans, scraped

2 tablespoons orange zest

2 to 3 drops orange food coloring

HOW TO MAKE IT

Cupcakes **1** Prepare the Vanilla Bean Cupcake batter according to the recipe directions, but leave out ⅛ cup of the milk and add ⅛ cup fresh orange juice instead. Add the orange zest with the dry ingredients. **2** Bake the cupcakes according to the recipe directions. **3** Mix together the simple syrup and the remaining 1 cup orange juice. **4** When the cupcakes are hot from the oven, heavily drench them with the syrup.

Frosting **1** Prepare the Vanilla American Buttercream according to the recipe directions. **2** Divide the buttercream in half. To one half, add the vanilla bean scrapings. **3** Add the orange zest to the other half of the buttercream and dye it slightly orange with the food coloring.

Put It All Together **1** Place both parts of the frosting side by side in your piping bag fitted with a star tip. I use a star tip, but for no particular reason. **2** Swirl the frosting on to the cupcakes—it'll naturally make the orange and white swirl beautifully together.

CHOC-O-MaTIC

★★★★★

Chocolate Decadence

This cupcake was formerly known as the Chocolate Slut, and I made it when I tried out for my job in Amsterdam, so I can't take credit for the name...but I got the job, so I must've done something right.

Cupcakes
1 recipe Devil's Food Cupcakes (page 19)

Frosting
1 recipe Ganache (page 30)

Put It All Together
1 recipe Chocolate Sauce (page 38)

¼ cup cocoa nibs (found at gourmet grocery stores or online)

HOW TO MAKE IT

Frosting **1** ***Start the day before***—Prepare the ganache according to the recipe directions.

Cupcakes **1** Prepare and bake the Devil's Food Cupcakes according to the recipe directions.

Put It All Together **1** Prepare the chocolate syrup according to the recipe directions. **2** With your index finger, poke holes in all the cupcakes and fill the holes with the chocolate syrup. **3** Frost the cupcakes with the ganache and top each one with the cocoa nibs.

THE SLASH

Really this cupcake is simple, but the little chocolate curls make it stand out. And yes, it's a nod to Slash, arguably one of the best guitarists of our time.

Cupcakes
1 recipe Devil's Food Cupcakes (page 19)

Frosting
1 recipe Vanilla American Buttercream (page 27)

Put It All Together
1 recipe Chocolate Curls (page 37)

HOW TO MAKE IT

Cupcakes **1** Prepare and bake the Devil's Food Cupcakes according to the recipe directions.

Frosting **1** Prepare the Vanilla American Buttercream according to the recipe directions.

Put It All Together **1** Prepare the chocolate curls according to the recipe directions. **2** Using a piping bag with a large round tip, place a big dollop of buttercream on each cupcake. **3** Lightly dip the tops of the cupcakes into the chocolate curls. You can mix this recipe up a bit by coloring or flavoring your frosting. I've used flavors like raspberry extract, peppermint extract, orange oil, and kirsch.

CHOCOLATE HAZELNUT

This may be the most popular nut-based cupcake I've ever made. Hazelnuts add a sweet fruitiness with a very smooth aftertaste and an air of sophistication, so this is an "impress the guest" and not so much a "feed the kids" kind of cupcake.

Cupcakes
1 recipe Devil's Food Cupcakes (page 19)

Frosting
2 cups raw hazelnuts, shelled, and peeled

¼ cup powdered sugar

1 recipe Chocolate American Buttercream (page 27)

Put It All Together
1 recipe Chocolate Curls (page 37)

2 tablespoons finely chopped toasted hazelnuts, for garnish

HOW TO MAKE IT

Cupcakes **1** Prepare and bake the Devil's Food Cupcakes according to the recipe directions.

Frosting **1** Preheat the oven to 350°F. Spread the hazelnuts in a single layer on the cookie sheet and toast them until you can smell them wafting from the oven. Set aside to cool. **2** Purée the cooled hazelnuts with the powdered sugar in a food processor until a peanut butter–like consistency is achieved. (To store this hazelnut butter, keep it at room temperature, but use it quickly or it will spoil.) **3** Prepare the Chocolate American Buttercream according to the recipe directions. **4** Fold ½ cup of the hazelnut butter into the buttercream.

Put It All Together **1** Prepare the chocolate curls according to the recipe directions. **2** Use your index finger to poke holes through the centers of all the cooled cupcakes. Spoon the remaining hazelnut butter into the holes. **3** Frost the cupcakes with the buttercream in a piping bag with a star tip and make a swirl to create height. **4** Sprinkle chopped, toasted hazelnuts over the frosting and top with a few chocolate curls.

Pumpkin Chocolate Spice

Hands down, fall is my favorite season with my favorite seasonal flavors. This cupcake is the embodiment of all that is awesome about this season. The classic combination of pumpkin and spices is made even better with the decadent addition of figs and chocolate ganache.

Cupcakes
¾ pound pumpkin
¼ cup butter or oil
2 teaspoons ground cinnamon
½ teaspoon ground nutmeg
½ teaspoon ground cloves
½ teaspoon ground allspice
1 recipe Devil's Food Cupcakes (page 19)

Frosting
1 recipe Ganache (page 30)

Put It All Together
1 (12-ounce) jar fig jam

HOW TO MAKE IT

Frosting **1** *Start the day before*—Prepare the ganache according to the recipe directions.

Cupcakes **1** Preheat the oven to 400°F. **2** Cut the pumpkins in half and place the halves face-down on the baking sheet. Wrap the whole thing in foil with the butter or oil and bake for about 1 hour. **3** When the pumpkins come out of the oven, remove the foil and allow them to cool. **4** Peel the pumpkins and dice them into ¼-inch cubes. You should end up with about 2 cups diced pumpkin. **5** Prepare the Devil's Food Cupcake batter, adding the cinnamon, nutmeg, cloves, and allspice to the batter with the dry ingredients. **6** Once the wet ingredients have been incorporated into the dry ingredients, fold in the pumpkin. **7** Bake the cupcakes according to the recipe directions.

Put It All Together **1** With your index finger, poke holes through the cupcakes and fill them with the fig jam. **2** Using a piping bag with a star tip, frost the cupcakes with the ganache and sprinkle each one with a little ground cloves.

Coffee and a Cigarette

Ahh, the name…if people don't know I'm referring to the chocolate cigarette on top of each cupcake, I usually get nasty looks. However, the name is a nod to all my pre-mom early mornings as a young pastry chef. Coffee and a cigarette—what a perfect pair. You can probably go to your local pastry shop and buy chocolate cigarettes; however, if you want to tackle this on your own, here's the easiest way.

Cupcakes
1 recipe Devil's Food Cupcakes (page 19)
2 tablespoons dry instant coffee grounds

Frosting
½ cup espresso beans (whatever your favorite are)
1 recipe Ganache (page 30)

Put It All Together
12 Chocolate Cigarettes (page 37)

HOW TO MAKE IT

Frosting **1** ***Start the day before***—Run the espresso beans through a food processor (or ask your local coffee shop for excess grounds that they tap out before they get used in drinks). **2** Begin preparing the ganache according to the recipe directions. When the cream comes to a boil, add the coffee. Remove the pan from the heat and let the mixture steep for about 20 minutes. **3** Strain the coffee grounds out of the cream with a very fine sieve or cheesecloth. **4** Bring the cream up to a boil again and pour it over the chocolate mixture. **5** Finish the ganache according to the recipe directions.

Cupcakes **1** Prepare the Devil's Food Cupcake batter according to the directions, and add the instant coffee grounds with the dry ingredients. **2** Bake the cupcakes according to the recipe directions.

Put It All Together **1** Prepare the chocolate cigarettes according to the recipe directions. If you have any leftover chocolate, you can dip espresso beans in it to use as garnish. **2** Frost the cooled cupcakes with the ganache and top each one with a chocolate cigarette and a chocolate-covered coffee bean, if you made them.

Chocolate Peanut Butter

I grew up in the peanut butter cup heyday, and that flavor combination has followed me for years. I just love it, and the funny thing is that my kids do, too. For this recipe, I use chunky peanut butter because it's my favorite, but you really can use any kind as long as it doesn't have added sugar...unless you want to be bouncing off the walls.

Cupcakes
1 recipe Devil's Food Cupcakes (page 19)

Frosting
1 recipe Vanilla American Buttercream (page 27)

1 cup peanut butter

HOW TO MAKE IT

Cupcakes **1** Prepare and bake the Devil's Food Cupcakes according to the recipe directions.

Frosting **1** Prepare the Vanilla American Buttercream according to the recipe directions, but use only ¼ cup of vegan margarine and mix in the peanut butter.

Put It All Together **1** Frost the cooled cupcakes with the peanut butter buttercream. **2** You can top them with a drizzle of chocolate or chopped, toasted peanuts.

CHOCOLATE GINGER

Chocolate and ginger are so amazing together. There are a lot of chocolate combinations that are classic and delicious, but ginger seems to just one-up all of its competition. We use ginger two ways in this recipe, but if it's too much, just take the ginger out of the ganache, or cut the amount in half completely.

Cupcakes
4 tablespoons chopped candied ginger
1 recipe Devil's Food Cupcakes (page 19)

Ganache
1 recipe Ganache (page 30)
2 tablespoons grated fresh ginger

Put It All Together
12 pieces candied ginger

HOW TO MAKE IT

Ganache **1** *Start the day before*—Prepare the ganache according to the recipe directions, but add the ginger to the cream as it heats up. **2** Once the cream has come to a simmer, remove it from the heat and allow the ginger to steep for 20 minutes. **3** Strain the ginger out and heat the cream again and pour it over the chocolate. **4** Finish making the ganache according to the recipe directions.

Cupcakes **1** Prepare the Devil's Food Cupcake batter according to the directions. **2** Fold the candied ginger into the batter. **3** Bake the cupcakes according to the recipe directions.

Put It All Together **1** Frost the cupcakes with the ganache using a piping bag with a star tip. **2** Top each cupcake with a candied ginger piece or a stripe of ground ginger.

Chocolate Raspberry

This cupcake is tied with the Chocolate Peanut Butter for being the most popular vegan cupcake we make. The flavors are classic but subtle and, most importantly, super delicious.

Cupcakes
1 recipe Devil's Food Cupcakes (page 19)

Frosting
1 recipe Vanilla American Buttercream (page 27)

1 cup raspberry jam

Put It All Together
2 cups raspberry jam

HOW TO MAKE IT

Cupcakes **1** Prepare and bake the Devil's Food Cupcakes according to the recipe directions.

Frosting **1** Prepare the Vanilla American Buttercream according to the recipe directions. **2** Fold your favorite raspberry jam into the buttercream.

Put It All Together **1** With your index finger, poke holes in all the cupcakes and fill the holes with the raspberry jam. **2** Frost the tops of the cupcakes with raspberry buttercream, and you're done.

My BLOODY VALENTINe

This cupcake is super simple but really delicious. It was, of course, highlighted as a Valentine's Day cupcake, but it has since been ordered for a lot of vampire-themed parties.

Cupcakes
1 recipe Devil's Food Cupcakes (page 19)

Frosting
1 recipe Chocolate American Buttercream (page 27)

Put It All Together
2 cups cherry jam (see note)

HOW TO MAKE IT

Cupcakes **1** Prepare and bake the Devil's Food Cupcakes according to the recipe directions.

Frosting **1** Prepare the Chocolate American Buttercream according to the recipe directions.

Put It All Together **1** With your index finger, poke holes in the tops of all the cupcakes and fill them with the cherry jam. **2** Frost the cupcakes with a swirl of the chocolate buttercream. **3** Top each cupcake with a teaspoon of drippy, runny cherry jam.

NOTE: Make sure to buy cherry jam, not jelly, with whole crushed cherries. You can also make your own filling by cooking down about 4 cups fresh cherries with about ½ cup sugar.

i WANT CaNDY

*****

SNICKERDOODLE

This one sort of speaks for itself. The flavor is very classic Americana and pleases both children and adults. I believe the trick to a good snickerdoodle is in the cinnamon itself. We get our Ceylon cinnamon ground fresh on a weekly basis to ensure it's super top quality.

Cupcakes
1 recipe Vanilla Bean Cupcakes (page 16)
4 tablespoons cinnamon

Frosting
1 recipe Italian Buttercream (page 24)

Put It All Together
2 tablespoons cinnamon
3 tablespoons raw sugar

HOW TO MAKE IT

Cupcakes **1** Prepare the Vanilla Bean Cupcake batter according to the recipe directions. Add the cinnamon with the dry ingredients. **2** Bake the cupcakes according to the recipe directions.

Frosting **1** Prepare the Italian Buttercream according to the recipe directions.

Put It All Together **1** Mix the cinnamon and sugar together in a small bowl. **2** Using a piping bag with a large round tip, put a big dollop of buttercream on top of each cupcake. **3** Dip the cupcakes upside down in the cinnamon-sugar topping.

CHOCOLATE TURTLE

Per customer request, the Chocolate Turtle came to life, but I'm not sure why we hadn't made it before. This cupcake was actually the flavor of our wedding cake and certainly is a favorite.

Cupcakes
1 recipe Devil's Food Cupcakes (page 19)

Candied Pecans
12 large pecans
3 egg whites
3 tablespoons sugar

Frosting
1 recipe Chocolate American Buttercream
(page 27)

Put It All Together
1 recipe All-Purpose Caramel (page 34)

HOW TO MAKE IT

Candied Pecans **1** Preheat the oven to 350°F. **2** Place the pecans in a medium bowl and drizzle them with the egg whites and sugar. Toss the mixture together and place pecans on a baking sheet. **3** Toast the pecans in the oven until they become dry, about 15 to 20 minutes. They'll still seem a little soft because of the heat, but they'll harden up as they cool.

Cupcakes **1** Prepare and bake the Devil's Food Cupcakes according to the recipe directions.

Frosting **1** Prepare the Chocolate American Buttercream according to the recipe directions.

Put It All Together **1** Prepare the caramel according to the recipe directions. **2** With your index finger, poke holes through the cooled cupcakes and fill them with the caramel. **3** Frost the cupcakes with the buttercream and drizzle caramel on top. **4** Top each cupcake with one candied pecan.

SaLtED CARAMEL AKA VERUCA SALT

We're lovers of the whole salty-sweet combination, and when we were asked to create a cupcake for "Girls Rock Chicago," this salted caramel recipe seemed to fit perfectly, mostly because of its name. However, it was so well received that several other organizations, like CHIRP independent radio, have asked us to make it to represent their charities as well.

Cupcakes
1 recipe Vanilla Bean Cupcakes (page 16)
¼ teaspoon fleur de sel (see note)
¼ teaspoon black lava salt (see note)
¼ teaspoon Hawaiian red salt (see note)
¼ teaspoon French gray salt (see note)

Frosting
1 recipe All-Purpose Caramel (page 34)
1 recipe Italian Buttercream (page 24)

HOW TO MAKE IT

Cupcakes **1** Prepare the Vanilla Bean Cupcake batter according to the recipe directions. **2** When the basic cupcake batter is finished, mix in all four salts. **3** Bake according to the recipe directions.

Frosting **1** Prepare the caramel according to the recipe directions and allow it to cool. **2** Prepare the Italian Buttercream according to the recipe directions. **3** Reserve half of the caramel (2 cups) for filling the cupcakes. Fold the remaining caramel into the buttercream.

Put It All Together **1** Poke holes through the cupcakes with your finger and fill them with the reserved caramel. We use a squeeze bottle to do this, but you can also use a spoon or a liquid measuring cup. **2** Using a piping bag with a star tip, frost the cupcakes with the buttercream. **3** Top the cupcakes with a pinch of the four salts for color.

NOTE: Specialty spice stores will have these salts. We buy ours at The Spice House, a small chain in the Midwest. You can also order their products online at www.thespicehouse.com.

PEPPERMINT CANDY

Originally we made this cupcake for a client who wanted a fire-and-ice-themed winter cupcake buffet. We sold the extra Peppermint Candy Cupcakes in the shop and they sold out, so we continued to make them throughout the holiday season. We bring them back now and then.

Cupcakes
1 recipe Devil's Food Cupcakes (page 19)

12 peppermint candies, crushed

Frosting
1 recipe Vanilla American Buttercream (page 27)

1 tablespoon peppermint extract

Put It All Together
about 4 drops red food coloring (or beet powder), to taste (see note)

peppermint candies, crushed, for garnish

HOW TO MAKE IT

Cupcakes **1** Prepare the Devil's Food Cupcake batter according to the recipe directions. **2** Fold the crushed peppermint candies into the batter. **3** Bake the cupcakes according to the recipe directions.

Frosting **1** Prepare the Vanilla American Buttercream according to the recipe directions, and add the peppermint extract when you add the vanilla extract.

Put It All Together **1** Divide the frosting in half and use the food coloring to dye one half red. **2** Place the two colors side by side in a piping bag with a star tip and swirl the frosting onto the cupcakes. **3** Top each cupcake with crushed peppermint candies.

NOTE: The color of red food coloring varies from brand to brand, so the amount you add will depend on how red you want your cupcakes to be. Organic colors don't bake as well as conventional ones (they turn brown), so the beet powder is a good alternative (and it's better for you), although it will alter the flavor of the cupcakes a little and they won't get as bright red as they would with conventional colors.

S'MORE

S'mores are quite a phenomenon. Everything we make that's called "s'mores" sells better than anything else. It's just amazing. This is our cupcake version. The graham cracker is a small element, but I think everything balances out really well.

Cupcakes
1 recipe Devil's Food Cupcakes (page 19)

Filling
1 recipe Ganache (page 30)

Frosting
1 recipe French Meringue (page 32)

Put It All Together
12 small graham cracker pieces

HOW TO MAKE IT

Filling **1** *Start the day before*—Prepare the ganache according to the recipe directions.

Cupcakes **1** Prepare and bake the Devil's Food Cupcakes according to the recipe directions.

Frosting **1** Prepare the French meringue according to the recipe directions.

Put It All Together **1** Poke holes through all the cupcakes with your index finger and fill the holes with the ganache, then dip the top of each cupcake in the ganache as well. **2** Fill a pastry bag fitted with a big round tip with the French meringue and top each cupcake with a big dollop of meringue. If your meringue seems too grainy, just calm it down by mixing it by hand with a rubber spatula for a few seconds. **3** With a crème brûlée torch, make the top of each meringue golden and top with a piece of graham cracker.

PEPPERMINT COOKIES AND CREAM

This one was an accident. We had a bit of peppermint frosting that was white, and without tasting it, I frosted a whole bunch of chocolate cupcakes. Later, I learned that it was peppermint—and it was delicious. I added bits of dried cupcake and fresh mint for texture, and it has been a hit ever since. Now I dye the frosting green so there are no more mishaps.

Cupcakes
1 recipe Devil's Food Cupcakes (page 19)

Frosting
1 recipe Vanilla American Buttercream (page 27)

1 tablespoon peppermint extract, or to taste (or according to the bottle's directions; see note)

4 tablespoons fresh mint, minced

HOW TO MAKE IT

Cupcakes **1** Prepare and bake the Devil's Food Cupcakes according to the recipe directions. **2** Once the cupcakes are cool, crumble two of the cupcakes onto a sheet pan and toast them in a 350°F oven for about 20 minutes. **3** Transfer the toasted pieces to a food processor and pulse them a few times to make crumbs. Set the crumbs aside to cool.

Frosting **1** Prepare the Vanilla American Buttercream according to the recipe directions and add the peppermint extract when you add the vanilla. **2** Fold the mint and the toasted cupcake crumbs into the buttercream. If you want, fold in a drop of green food coloring.

Put It All Together **1** Use a piping bag with a star tip to frost the cupcakes. You can leave them as is or top them with a few leftover cupcake crumbs.

NOTE: There are amazing, nonchemical peppermint extracts out there. Try to find one that is still clear and not too syrupy. Nielsen Massey is my favorite.

CaRAMEL CORN

I always have fun using up spare ingredients to invent new cupcakes, and this one was really a hit. These cupcakes cannot be refrigerated, so you need to make them the day of consumption, but they seem to fill that human need for salty, sweet, smooth, and crunchy.

Cupcakes
1 recipe Devil's Food Cupcakes (page 19)

Frosting
1 recipe Ganache (page 30)

Put It All Together
caramel corn, preferably artisan-style from a
local bakery or candy maker

HOW TO MAKE IT

Frosting **1** *Start the day before*—Prepare the ganache according to the recipe directions.

Cupcakes **1** Prepare and bake the Devil's Food Cupcakes according to the recipe directions.

Put It All Together **1** Place a big dollop of the ganache on top of each cupcake. **2** Dip the cupcakes into the caramel corn face down. Make sure the caramel corn sticks to the entire top.

DIRT

Well, I love the band, but I suppose that has nothing to do with the cupcake itself. We actually developed this recipe for Earth Day. You can do a lot of renditions of it, like dyeing the pastry cream red instead of making it chocolate or having a gummy worm inside.

Cupcakes
1 recipe Devil's Food Cupcakes (page 19)

Frosting
1 recipe Ganache (page 30)

Chocolate Pastry Cream
1 recipe Pastry Cream (page 40)

1 cup melted dark chocolate (64% cocoa content or higher)

HOW TO MAKE IT

Frosting **1** *Start the day before*—Prepare the ganache according to the recipe directions.

Chocolate Pastry Cream **1** Prepare the pastry cream according to the recipe directions. **2** Whisk the melted chocolate into the warm pastry cream.

Cupcakes **1** Prepare and bake the Devil's Food Cupcakes according to the recipe directions. Allow the cupcakes to cool. **2** Preheat the oven to 325°F. **3** Take two of the baked cupcakes and smoosh them up to make crumbs. Toast those crumbs on a baking sheet in the oven for about 20 minutes to dry them out. **4** Let the crumbs cool and then pulse them 3 or 4 times in a blender.

Put It All Together **1** With your index finger, poke holes through the centers of the cupcakes and fill the holes with the chocolate pastry cream. **2** Using a piping bag with a big round tip, dollop the top of each cupcake with the ganache. **3** Dip the whole cupcake face down into the "dirt" cupcake crumbs, and you're done.

COOKIE DOUGH

This new rendition of a delicious classic is just what we needed to keep the cookie dough craze alive. The cookie dough is vegan, so you don't have to fumble around finding pasteurized eggs.

Cupcakes
1 recipe Vanilla Bean Cupcakes (page 16)

Frosting
1 recipe Vanilla American Buttercream (page 27)

Cookie Dough
1 cup palm fruit shortening

½ cup vegan margarine (like Earth Balance)

2 cups sugar

1 tablespoon vanilla extract

3 cups all-purpose flour

1 tablespoon salt

2 cups chocolate chips

HOW TO MAKE IT

Cupcakes **1** Prepare and bake the Vanilla Bean Cupcakes according to the recipe directions.

Cookie Dough **1** In the bowl of a standing mixer with the paddle attachment, starting at low speed and slowly increasing to high, combine the palm fruit shortening, vegan margarine, sugar, and vanilla and mix until light and fluffy, about 10 to 15 minutes. **2** Add the flour, salt, and chocolate chips. Mix on medium speed until the ingredients all come together. If it needs moisture, add soymilk until it gets to a cookie dough consistency.

Frosting **1** Prepare the Vanilla American Buttercream according to the recipe directions. **2** Set aside about a quarter of the basic buttercream. You'll only need three quarters for this recipe. **3** Mix the remaining buttercream with half the cookie dough with your hands. Let the cookie dough stay in little chunks, but nothing huge because it won't fit through a piping bag.

Put It All Together **1** With your hands, form the remaining cookie dough into little gumball-sized balls and stuff one into the center of each cupcake. **2** Frost the cupcakes with the cookie dough frosting and top each one with chocolate chips.

SHUT YOUr PIE HOLe

*****

BLACKBERRY PEACH CRUMBLE

This quintessential farmer's market cupcake uses the best fruit at the peak of the season.

Cupcakes
2 whole ripe peaches

3 tablespoons sugar

1 recipe Vanilla Bean Cupcakes (page 16)

1 cup blackberries, chopped

Frosting
1 recipe French Meringue (page 32)

Streusel Topping
2 tablespoons raw sugar

4 tablespoons flour

2 tablespoons butter or soy margarine (to keep it vegan)

HOW TO MAKE IT

Cupcakes **1** Preheat the oven to 350°F. **2** Pit and slice the peaches, leaving the skins on. Toss the slices in the sugar on a baking sheet, and bake for about 20 minutes until the peaches are soft and bright orange. Let the peaches cool in their juices. **3** Prepare the Vanilla Bean Cupcake batter according to the recipe directions. **4** Chop the peaches, leaving the skins on, into little bite-sized pieces. Toss them together with the chopped blackberries, and then fold all the fruit into the batter. **5** Bake the cupcakes according to the recipe directions.

Streusel Topping **1** Preheat the oven to 350°F. **2** In a bowl, mix the sugar, flour, and butter with your fingers until the topping is mealy in texture, but with some pea-sized pieces left. **3** Bake the mixture on a baking sheet for about 15 minutes. **4** Let the streusel cool and then break it up with your fingers.

Frosting **1** Prepare the French meringue according to the recipe directions.

Put It All Together **1** Using a piping bag with a medium star tip, place three big, spiky dollops of French meringue on each cupcake. **2** Sprinkle the toasted streusel on top of the meringue and you're done.

CaRRoT CaKE

OK, so I love carrot cake—I have no idea why, but I just do—and I hate coconut. Hate is a strong word, and I believe that coconut may be the only thing I really hate (except racists). However, this carrot cake recipe is awesome and uses coconut perfectly. We've had some pretty discerning people who say this is the best carrot cake they've had, and it's most popular with our wholesale customers.

Cupcakes

1 pound canned crushed pineapple

1⅓ cups sugar

1 cup all-purpose flour

1 tablespoon baking soda

1 teaspoon cinnamon

¼ teaspoon nutmeg

¼ teaspoon salt

½ cup sunflower oil

4 eggs

4 cups grated carrot

Frosting

1 recipe Cream Cheese Frosting (page 28)

HOW TO MAKE IT

Cupcakes **1** Strain the pineapple. Set up the strainer so the juice goes into the sink (or you can save the liquid to drink, but just make sure to set up a bowl under the strainer first). Place the crushed pineapple into the strainer. Let it strain the entire time you're measuring and mixing the batter so enough liquid will be gone that it won't weigh the batter down. **2** Preheat the oven to 350°F and line a cupcake pan with cupcake liners. **3** Place the sugar, flour, baking soda, cinnamon, nutmeg, and salt in the mixing bowl and mix together with a whisk. **4** Add the oil, eggs, pineapple, and carrots while mixing with a spoon or rubber spatula. This batter will be pretty stiff. **5** With the ice cream scoop, fill the cups in the cupcake pan about ¾ full and bake for about 15 to 20 minutes. The tops will feel spongy and will spring back when they're done.

Frosting **1** Prepare the Cream Cheese Frosting according to the recipe directions.

Put It All Together **1** Using a piping bag with a star tip, frost the cooled cupcakes with the frosting.

NOTE: If you don't use this cupcake batter right away, it'll become more liquidy, but don't worry about it. Just make sure that if you store it, you mix it again before baking or your cupcakes will be inconsistent.

German Chocolate

This cupcake is super delicious and seems to sell best in the wintertime, for obvious reasons. It's pretty classic, but has stayed on the menu for good reason. Sometimes you just need comfort—and this is comfort.

Cupcakes
1 recipe Chocolate Sponge Cupcakes
(page 22)

German Chocolate Filling
1 cup half-and-half

1 cup brown sugar

¼ cup butter

½ teaspoon salt

Frosting
1 recipe Ganache (page 30)

3 egg yolks

1 cup toasted chopped pecans

2 cups desiccated (dried and shredded, no sugar added) coconut

HOW TO MAKE IT

Frosting **1** *Start the day before*—Prepare the ganache according to the recipe directions.

German Chocolate Filling **1** In a medium-sized, thick-bottomed soup or saucepan over medium heat, combine the half-and-half, brown sugar, butter, salt, and egg yolks. Stir the mixture until it comes to a boil. **2** Let the mixture boil for about 2 minutes, then strain it through a sieve and into a mixing bowl. **3** Stir the pecans and coconut into the filling mixture and allow it to cool.

Cupcakes **1** Prepare and bake the Chocolate Sponge Cupcakes according to the recipe directions.

Put It All Together **1** With your index finger, poke a hole through each cupcake and fill the holes with the German Chocolate Filling. **2** Frost each cupcake with the ganache and a little extra dollop of the filling.

LeMON MERiNGUE

Really, it couldn't get more classic than this, and when it's done right, it's fabulous. The texture of the meringue needs to be perfect and you'll rock any party with these cupcakes.

Cupcakes
1 recipe Lemon Cupcakes (page 23)
½ cup lemon juice
1 recipe Simple Syrup (page 44)

Frosting
1 recipe French Meringue (page 32)

Put It All Together
1 recipe Lemon Curd (page 39)

HOW TO MAKE IT

Cupcakes **1** Prepare and bake the Lemon Cupcakes according to the recipe directions. **2** Add the lemon juice to the Simple Syrup. **3** When the cupcakes are hot from the oven, brush the tops with the syrup.

Frosting **1** Prepare the French meringue according to the recipe directions.

Put It All Together **1** Prepare the lemon curd according to the recipe directions. **2** Poke holes through the centers of the cupcakes with your index finger. Fill the holes with lemon curd. **3** Top the cupcakes with big dollops of meringue. If you have a crème brûlée torch, you can slightly burn the meringue—it adds great flavor.

TIRAMISU

Obviously, tiramisu is as classic and delicious as it gets, but since I don't own an Italian bakery, I focus on local and regional American flavors. However, the number of people who ask me for tiramisu is amazing, so I decided to offer this cupcake as a tiramisu alternative.

Cupcakes
1 recipe Chocolate Sponge Cupcakes
(page 22)

2 cups mascarpone cheese

2 tablespoons dry instant coffee

½ cup dark rum

Ganache
½ cup espresso beans (whatever your favorite are)

1 recipe Ganache (page 30)

Frosting
1 recipe Vanilla American Buttercream
(page 27)

2 cups mascarpone cheese

2 vanilla beans

HOW TO MAKE IT

Ganache **1** *Start the day before*—Run the espresso beans through a food processor (or ask your local coffee shop for excess grounds that they tap out before they get used in drinks). **2** Bring the cream for the ganache to a boil and add the coffee. Remove the pan from the heat and let the mixture steep for about 20 minutes. **3** Strain the coffee grounds out of the cream through a very fine sieve or cheesecloth. **4** Bring the cream to a boil again and pour it over the chocolate mixture, then finish the ganache according to the recipe directions.

Cupcakes **1** Prepare the Chocolate Sponge Cupcake batter according to the recipe directions. **2** Mix the mascarpone cheese into the cupcake batter by hand. Squeeze it in your hand and swirl it into the batter, leaving larger chunks and smaller chunks. **3** Mix in the instant coffee with a rubber spatula. **4** Bake the cupcakes according to the recipe directions. **5** When they come out of the oven, heavily soak the cupcakes in the dark rum.

Frosting **1** Prepare the Vanilla American Buttercream according to the recipe directions. **2** Soften the mascarpone in the microwave on high power for a few seconds until it's soft and spreadable but not melted and warm. **3** With a rubber spatula, mix the cheese and the vanilla scrapings into the frosting until incorporated.

Put It All Together **1** With your index finger, poke holes in the rum-soaked cupcakes and fill the holes with the espresso ganache. **2** Frost the cupcakes with the mascarpone buttercream. Top each one with a sprinkling of cocoa powder or chocolate-covered espresso beans.

Bananas Foster

The very first dish I ever had to pretend I knew how to cook to impress a chef I wanted to work for was bananas foster on a hot-line buffet. Being a big fan of liquor, I think I did a great job, but I don't remember if I was hired or not. Anyhow, this cupcake is in memory of my early years when I was still trying to get my footing in this industry.

Cupcakes
4 bananas
¼ cup butter
½ cup sugar
2 tablespoons vanilla extract
1 vanilla bean
1 cup rum
1 recipe Vanilla Bean Cupcakes (page 16)

Frosting
1 recipe Vanilla American Buttercream (page 27)
1 cup brown sugar

Streusel Topping
2 tablespoons raw sugar
4 tablespoons flour
½ cup pecans
2 tablespoons butter or soy margarine (to keep it vegan)

Put It All Together
1½ cups rum

HOW TO MAKE IT

Cupcakes **1** Slice the bananas into ¼-inch coins. Melt the butter in a sauté pan and add the banana slices. **2** Sauté the bananas for about 1 minute on each side, keeping the pieces moving, then sprinkle them with the sugar and add the vanilla extract. Throw in the whole vanilla bean cut in half and scraped, including the pod, and pour in the rum. The pan may flame up a little, so be VERY careful. Once the flame goes down, the alcohol has evaporated. Then pour out contents onto a baking sheet to cool. **3** Prepare the Vanilla Bean Cupcake batter according to the recipe directions. **4** Once the banana mixture is cool, remove the vanilla bean pod and fold the bananas into the batter. **5** Bake the cupcakes according to the recipe directions.

Frosting **1** Prepare the Vanilla American Buttercream according to the recipe directions. **2** Fold the brown sugar into the buttercream.

Streusel Topping **1** Preheat the oven to 350°F. **2** In a bowl, mix the sugar, flour, pecans, and butter together with your fingers until the topping is mealy in texture, but with some pea-sized pieces left. **3** Bake the mixture on a baking sheet in the oven for about 15 minutes. **4** Let the streusel cool and then break it up with your fingers.

Put It All Together **1** With a pastry brush, heavily soak the cupcakes in the rum. **2** Frost the cupcakes with the brown sugar buttercream. **3** Top each cupcake with the streusel topping.

CONVERSIOns

HANDY CONVERSIONS

1 tablespoon	3 teaspoons
1 cup	16 tablespoons
1 pint	2 cups
1 quart	2 pints
1 gallon	4 quarts
1 pound	16 ounces
1 stick butter	½ cup / 8 ounces
1 ounce butter	2 tablespoons

METRIC CONVERSIONS

1 teaspoon	5 milliliters
1 tablespoon	15 milliliters
1 cup	240 milliliters
2 cups	470 milliliters
4 cups	0.95 liter
4 quarts	3.8 liters
1 fluid ounce	30 milliliters / 28 grams
1 ounce	28 grams
1 pound	454 grams
350°F / 400°F	175°F / 200°C

About the Authors

MICHELLE AND VINNY GARCIA opened Bleeding Heart Bakery in Chicago in 2004 with the mission of providing thought-provoking pastry as delicious and beautiful as it is cutting edge. In late 2009, they opened a second Chicago location. They are also the owners of Smash Cake, a kid-focused bakery, also in Chicago. Michelle was named ACF region pastry chef of the year in 2006, and Bleeding Heart Bakery has won many awards, including Top Bakery in Chicago by *Chicago* magazine, and was named one of the top ten bakeries in the nation by an online poll. Veteran contestants on *Food Network Challenge*, Michelle and Vinny have competed in numerous cake contests. They live in Chicago.

About the Photographer

BILL LAMBERT is a Chicago-based freelance photographer specializing in food photography. He has been the Bleeding Heart Bakery's exclusive food photographer for three years. His work has been featured in *Modern Baking*, *Pastry & Baking North America*, *Chicago* magazine, *RedEye* Chicago, and *This is Why You're Fat*. He lives in Chicago with his wife, Peggy, and two children, Samantha and Gabrielle. You can find him online at www.twitter.com/chibill and www.ericksondesign.com.